Creating Interfaith Community

R. Marston Speight

Study Guide by
Glory and Jacob Dharmaraj

General Board of Global Ministries
The United Methodist Church
New York, New York

Creating Interfaith Community copyright © 2003 General Board of Global Ministries
A publication of the General Board of Global Ministries, The United Methodist Church

ISBN#1-890569-56-9

CONTENTS

ACKNOWLEDGMENTS

In preparing to write this book I interviewed a number of people at length. In gratitude for the information and insight they provided I am happy to name them here: Ghita Blackman, Amarjit Singh Buttar, Kenneth Dusyn, Malou Dusyn, James Friedman, Richard B. Griffis, Padam C. Jain, Ruth Martin, Shyamala Raman, Seth Riemer, Robert Saunders, Katherine Sebastian (Wataswan), Roy Sebastian (Chief Hockeo Running Deer), and Britt Williams.

I have reworked and incorporated into this book several passages from my publication, *Christian-Muslim Relations: An Introduction for Christians in the United States of America* (Hartford: Office on Christian-Muslim Relations, The National Council of the Churches of Christ in the U.S.A., 1983, reprinted, 1984 and 1986).

R. Marston Speight
Cromwell, Connecticut

What does the book title mean?

Some years ago I visited a large Egyptian town in the company of several friends from the Middle Eastern churches. We were observing the social service work done by members of the Coptic Evangelical Church of Egypt. After an evening visit to a literacy class in the church, we received word that a close relative of the town's mayor had been killed that day in an auto accident. The mayor was a Muslim, as were most of the inhabitants of that town. We decided that as a sign of our sympathy we should go to the mayor's house and offer our condolences. We went there and were ushered into the dimly lit atrium of the mayor's home. We sat down and were offered a cup of coffee. Then from another room we heard someone reciting the Koran in a melodious voice, which is the Muslim custom at such times of bereavement.

We talked quietly among ourselves for a little and all of a sudden the voice from the other room became silent. Then the recitation began again, this time on a different tone and with different words. Soon we Christians smiled to one another and felt the warmth of companionship with our Muslim hosts. The Koran reciter, advised of our presence in the house, had changed to a different chapter of the Muslims' holy book and had begun to declaim the story of Mary the mother of Jesus as contained in Surat Maryam (the Chapter of Mary). In those few minutes they, the Muslims, and we, the Christians, had created an experience of life together, interacting with each other on the basis of our faith. We were given the grace of a brief but intense moment of interfaith community, which is the subject of this book.

Everyone knows what community means, and no one doubts its importance. Wherever people live and interact together, sharing their common interests and concerns, making an effort to reach goals that make life worthwhile, there is community. It can exist at the workplace, in the neighborhood, in the church, and at school—almost everywhere that people get together socially. But this book deals with a type of community that is not so common in the U.S. *Interfaith community means life shared by believers from more than one religion who are inspired by their faith to such a shared experience.* This kind of community can exist in an organized long-term situation, for example, where Christians and Jews work together to settle refugees in a new country. Or such community can be of a briefer, passing nature like the experience that I had in the Egyptian home. A conference of Muslims, Hindus, Christians, and Jews to discuss the problem of religious hate crimes in a certain locality can be an experience of interfaith community. The essential elements in such a life experience are: (1) the participants act and relate to one another because of their faith; (2) and they retain their own religious beliefs and practices without giving up anything of their religion's distinctiveness.

The community we are talking about is in fact interfaith or interreligious, signifying "between religions," not interdenominational or "between churches." It is quite a different experience from the long-standing practice of denominations that organize interchurch councils or hold interdenominational Thanksgiving services or consult with one another about the possibilities of church union. Interfaith community introduces us to a new dimension of life: the possibility of reaching out to people of other religious faiths and seeking community with them.

Through much of North American church history, Christians have been fairly oblivious to the presence of other religions in our land. But today the other faiths have become so numerous and so prominent on the North American scene that we cannot ignore them. Our Christian brothers and sisters in other lands have had much more experience in living with believers of other religions than we have. They can help us to understand what interfaith community involves, and they can teach us the danger of neglecting the possibilities for such community.

The "creating" called for in the title of this book is our effort. We must do it, if it is to be done. Of course, the "we" involves more than ourselves. Interfaith community cannot exist without reciprocity. Everyone from the different religious groups involved must be agreed for it to succeed. And we cannot speak or act for the others. However, Christianity is the majority religion in our land, and as the larger group it seems appropriate, out of courtesy, at least, that we should take some initiative in undertaking interfaith community. Even if at first there is little or no response from the other faiths, a unilateral initiative on our part can help to prepare the way for eventual interfaith community. And what if believers from another religion come to us seeking peaceable, constructive relations on the basis of our respective faiths? Are we ready to respond in a friendly, helpful way? This book should help us to be Christians equal to the challenge of religious diversity in the United States.

In the first chapter I will describe some of the different religions that are at home in our country. After that some reasons for creating interfaith community will be given. Then will follow, in chapter 3, an exploration of some of the resources in Christian faith that can help us in responding to the multiplicity of faiths in our society. A number of interfaith communities exist already, in a variety of forms. Some of them constitute the subject of chapter 4, and the book concludes with some practical suggestions for creating interfaith community.

THE SHEMA OR CONFESSION OF FAITH

Hear, O Israel, the Lord is our God, the Lord is One. Blessed be the Name of His glorious kingdom forever and ever. And you shall love the Lord your God with all your heart and with all your soul and with all your might. And these words that I command you today shall be in your heart. And you shall teach them diligently to your children, and you shall speak of them when you sit at home, and when you walk along the way, and when you lie down and when you rise up. And you shall bind them as a sign on your hand, and they shall be for frontlets between your eyes. And you shall write them on the doorposts of your house and on your gates.

—Deuteronomy 6:4-9

1

RELIGION IN NORTH AMERICAN SOCIETY

In order to grasp the religious diversity of the U.S., consider one fairly typical city and the religions represented there. The place I have chosen is Hartford, Connecticut, one of the oldest cities in New England, situated halfway between Boston and New York City. Hartford is medium-sized, with about 120,000 people, but it has a metropolitan population of roughly 700,000. Greater Hartford has long exerted strong influence in the business, industrial, and cultural life of the nation. It is not noted as a religious center, but I daresay the religious bodies found there are typical of those found in most cities, large and small, of this nation.

To make this chapter manageable and so as not to confuse readers with too much detail, we decided to limit the description of religions to the following: Judaism, Islam, Baha'ism, Hinduism, Jainism, Sikhism, and Buddhism. Some of these may not be among the largest groups in the Hartford area, but they are ones that have already expressed interest in creating interfaith community and they all belong to large bodies worldwide. At the end of the chapter is a short discussion of Native American religions.

If we open the yellow pages of the telephone directory, we should find listed most of the religious communities in Hartford. But where do we find them in the telephone book? Not under "religion," although a few might be listed as "religious organizations." To find the different faiths listed we must turn to "churches," and this is a sign of how the Christian majority dominates even the listing of religions in the telephone directory.

After all, "churches" is purely a Christian word. There, under that heading, we find all of the numerous Christian bodies in Hartford, the old established denominations, the diverse more recent ones, and other faiths that are either offshoots of traditional churches or new religions altogether. Most of these names are not our concern here. Picking our way through the subheadings under "churches," we find "Buddhist Pagoda" and "Muhammad Islamic Center" among the entries.

Before we go on to specific religious groups, let me call attention to the question of language. Nearly every religion depends heavily on a language foreign to English to express its beliefs and describe its practices. This religious language poses a barrier to understanding by outsiders. To one seeking fundamental information about another faith, the use of foreign terms is confusing. So I am deliberately avoiding, as much as possible, the use of special foreign religious language in this sketch of other religions. For example, Jews depend on the Hebrew tongue, and with the flourishing of the Jewish State of Israel, that language has enjoyed increased use and importance. Readers should go to more detailed books to find the special vocabulary of a particular faith.

JUDAISM

Prayer for Celebration of the Shabbat at Home

Blessed are You, Lord, our God, King of the Universe, who sanctifies us with His commandments, and has been pleased with us. You have lovingly and willingly given us Your holy Shabbat as an inheritance, in memory of creation. The Shabbat is the first among our holy days, and a remembrance of our exodus from Egypt. Indeed, You have chosen us and made us holy among all peoples and have willingly and lovingly given us Your holy Shabbat for an inheritance. Blessed are You, who sanctified the Shabbat. Amen.

—The Kiddush

Back in the telephone directory, we find that one religion entry has broken free of the confusing heading, "churches." To find telephone numbers for Jewish places of worship, one must turn to "synagogues." This autonomy of Jews in the yellow pages is a sign of their numerical importance in Hartford, and, even more, it points to the fact that Jews are the oldest religious minority in that city, having begun to settle there in colonial times. In the neighborhoods of greater Hartford you will find about 40 synagogues in all, as well as community centers, health and elder care centers, and schools, all to serve a vibrant population of around 26,000 Jews. Jews, the most numerous of minority religions in the U.S., are in fact relatively few in number worldwide, about 13 million. They are found in all sectors of the business, professional, and cultural

These Orthodox Jews are praying at the Western Wall in Jerusalem.

life of the area. Programs of Jewish studies in colleges and universities serve the needs of scholars. In a secular sense we can say that Jews are assimilated in the larger community of Hartford. But religiously they stand apart, belonging to a unique tradition of faith and practice that goes back 4,000 years to the Middle East, out of which region their people and their beliefs emerged. They trace their roots to Abraham, who brought his people to faith in one God. Then as the children of Abraham continued their walk of faith under the leadership of Moses and a line of kings and prophets, a nation was formed, a law was divinely revealed, a land was settled, and authoritative writings of legislation, history, and devotion developed. This nation,

called Israel, felt a sense of destiny as a collective witness to the reality of the one God of the universe. At various times it came into conflict with secular powers and rival religious movements. Internal strife also caused serious breaks at times in the unity of the nation. Over the centuries the people of Israel were scattered into many countries, but they have always retained their ethnic and religious distinctiveness. In fact ethnicity is just as important as faith in identifying Jews. Today the descendants of Moses' people who find themselves in Greater Hartford enjoy a rich heritage handed down to them from many generations of Jews who have maintained the tradition in spite of untold hardship and persecution. They, along with nearly six million other Jews in the U.S., thrive in the atmosphere of freedom in this country.

History is the primary scene in which Jewish life works itself out. The pages of the Hebrew Scripture, known to Christians as the Old Testament, recount the story of a people specially chosen to show forth the beauty and power of life lived by faith in the Creator of all things, the one true and living God. This unique One whom Jews worship is understood to relate to humanity in personal ways, so that certain similarities between the divine and the human exist. Nevertheless, the divine Lord is always regarded as being infinitely high above all that is created, always other than human beings. The particular calling of the Jewish nation is expressed as a divine-human agreement, or "covenant." This agreement was inaugurated by the giving of the Ten Commandments, which became to Jews the basis of their life. They are not as concerned about delving into the mystery of

To celebrate Rosh Hashanah, these Reformed Jews sound the Shofar in New York City.

God's nature as they are in regulating their lives to conform to the models of behavior set forth in divinely inspired laws and teachings. Besides the Bible, they revere the Talmud, a collection of oral traditions, written down concerning all aspects of Jewish practice and experience.

History as it continues to unfold teaches Jews further lessons of their faith. Dispersed to all parts of the earth, they have seen their own in Europe suffer the ultimate in horror at the hands of Nazi Germany during World War II. While the persecutions leading up to those tragic events were gathering force, from the remnant of the dispersion emerged a dynamic movement called Zionism to regain the Promised Land for Jews. Its result has been the establishment of the State of Israel, an event of great hope to all people of that faith. The lessons of history have been sad beyond measure for Jews, and though the present scene of Israel's rebirth as a nation offers promise, Jews are cautious and watchful. Anti-Jewish feeling lies just below the surface in many cultures. At a Jewish-Christian dialogue in Middletown, Connecticut, Rabbi Seth Riemer of Congregation Adath Israel joined several of his coreligionists in expressing their apprehension regarding signs of prejudice and animosity toward Jews on the international scene.

Judaism anticipates history. Jewish faith has nourished through the centuries the hope of a golden age when a divinely appointed leader called the messiah, or anointed one, will rule the world in peace. While many Jews today do not hold to a literal interpretation of their ancient messianic belief, it remains as a symbol to encourage hope in a world community founded on the promise of universal justice.

Worship by Jews can be understood as a vast meditation upon the historical unfolding of their life as a people. Whether in the home, traditionally the primary place for learning and practicing Jewish values, or in the synagogue, each week they observe Shabbat (the Sabbath), a solemn day of rest, prayer, and praise to the Almighty. When the people gather, they follow the leadership of a rabbi, or teacher. There is a public reading from the Torah, the Bible's first five books, held most sacred by Jews. Praying, litanies, songs, chants, and sermons are also parts of the weekly service. The atmosphere in the synagogue may vary from respectful dignity to joyful exuberance.

Jews also commemorate historical events of their faith by celebrating festivals. The Sabbath itself is one of them, commemorating the week of divine creation of the world. Among other occasions is the yearly observance of Passover, or the time when Moses' people were delivered from slavery in Egypt. The Feast of Weeks is a harvest festival as well a remembrance of the giving of the divine law. On the Feast of Tabernacles, the people remember God's protection during ancient Israel's wanderings in the wilderness on the way to the Promised Land.

Because God in Judaism is holy and infinitely just, the standards of that faith for morals and ethics are high. Believers hold to certain ceremonial rules regarding rites of initiation, food, drink, dress, and social behavior, rules that are observed with varying strictness. In the U.S., Jews have divided into several denominations, the largest of which are the Orthodox, the Conservative, and the Reform branches. Differences between them have to do both with ritual practices and with beliefs, although in Judaism it is difficult to separate one from the other. Historically, Jews believe that God is intimately involved in the affairs of the world and that creation has a moral purpose in which good is rewarded and evil is punished. Besides being perfectly just and righteous, God is also gracious and merciful, extending pardon to all who repent of their misdoings.

It is obvious that Christians have much in common with Jews. Both go back to the same roots of faith and acknowledge the same holy Scriptures, although Christians add the New Testament to make up their Bible. The main difference between Judaism and Christianity is that whereas for Jews the messiah is yet to come, Christians believe that he has come in the person of Jesus, son of Mary. Practically all other differences, major and minor, can be interpreted in terms of this basic historical and theological divergence.

The Opening

In the name of God, the Merciful, the Compassionate. Praise be to God, the Lord of the worlds, the Merciful, the Compassionate, Master of the Day of Judgment. You alone we worship; You alone we ask for help. Show us the straight path, the path of those whom you have favored, not the path of those who have incurred your wrath or who have gone astray.

—The Koran

Differences in Religious Communities

We have revealed Scripture to you with truth, confirming and safeguarding previously revealed Scriptures…. To each one [of the religious communities] we have given a law and a way. If God had willed he would have made all of you one community. But, that which you have has been given you so that he might test you thereby. Outdo one another, then, in good deeds, turning, all of you, toward God your goal. Finally he will let you know how you differed from each other.

—The Koran

Men and boys at noon prayers at a mosque in Brunei.

Adherents to Islam are called Muslims. They make up a community in Greater Hartford of several thousand believers. In 2002, according to one report, when all Connecticut Muslims were invited to celebrate together the festival of the breaking of the month-long yearly fast, approximately 10,000 people gathered at a public arena. Although exact statistics are hard to come by for such an ethnically diverse group, it is estimated that the total population in Connecticut may be near 25,000. Muslims, of multiple ethnic origins, number well over one billion people in the world. Nearly one person in five across the earth belongs to the religion of Islam.

Muslims believe in one God, Creator of all things, unique in life, power, mercy, and justice. The revelation of this God came in the seventh century after Christ to an Arabian trader named Muhammad. He passed the message on to others and headed a community of those who gave up the worship of idols and spirits. The revelations that Muhammad received were believed to have come directly from God. Eventually they were put together in a book called the Koran, which was written in the Arabic language. Besides the holy Scripture of the Koran, Muslims hold as authoritative a large collection of reports telling about the Prophet Muhammad's interpretations of the Koran, his actions in everyday life, and his attitudes. These reports are called *hadith*.

Muslims place themselves directly in the line of those who worship one God, so they feel kinship with Jews and Christians. They believe, however, that Muhammad came to complete or seal the line of prophets whom God sent into the world as guidance for humankind. The prophetic line began with the first man, Adam, and included many of those named in the Bible, such as Abraham, Moses, and Jesus. Muslims believe God gave Scriptures to Moses and to Jesus and that in their true interpretation they agree with the message of the Koran.

Islam sets forth the duties for human life in a clear way. Life has serious purpose as a response in faith to the creative and sustaining power of the Almighty. A Muslim's life is one of social responsibility. In this respect, Christians can feel quite at home with the moral standards of Islam.

Muslims also hold that the final goal for life lies beyond the brief span of years spent on earth. After death there will be a new life. The same God who created the world will also call forth in resurrection all who have died. Then perfect justice will be administered. Righteous living will be rewarded and wickedness punished.

Every Friday at noon, Hartford Muslims, like their coreligionists everywhere, gather for communal prayer. Although the prayers can be held in any kind of room or hall, eight special buildings, or mosques, have been built or adapted for worship in Hartford. Originally the mosques served particular ethnic groups, such as Pakistanis, Arabs, Indonesians, Malays, African Americans, Iranians, etc., but now the worshipers come from all national backgrounds. Outwardly, except for one, the mosques are scarcely distinguishable from surrounding buildings. The prayer room is bare of furniture, the floor covered with carpets. Worshipers leave their shoes at the door and gather facing in the direction of Mecca, Arabia, where Islam began, the men in one group and the women in another. They stand in rows close together to carry out the ritual acts of prayer, its gestures, prostrations, recitations, and periods of silence. Worshipers follow the leadership of a person called the *imam*. They may also listen to chanting of the Koran and to the preaching of a sermon while seated on the floor. The ritual prayer of Islam is mostly in the form of praise to the Almighty, although petition does have a place. Prayer is performed at five fixed times each day, although communal worship is required only once a week. The language used is Arabic, but some petitions and the sermon are expressed in English.

Prayer as described above is the second of the five main practices of Islam, called "pillars" of the faith. The first pillar is the verbal confession, or witness, "I testify that there is no deity but God, and I testify that Muhammad is God's messenger." Another pillar is the obligatory contribution to charity, 2½ percent of one's total assets, given every year as an act of worship and of self-purification. The fourth basic practice is a month-long yearly fast from all food and drink during the daylight hours. And finally Muslims are required, health and wealth permitting, to make a pilgrimage to Mecca at least once in their lifetime. Mecca, in Arabia, is connected not only with the life of the Prophet Muhammad, but also, and even more importantly for the pilgrimage, with Abraham, the spiritual father of Muslims. As can be imagined, each of these pillars of Islam is full of multiple meanings and deserves to be explored by readers of this book as they get to know their Muslim neighbors.

Two main festivals highlight the calendar of Islam. One comes at the end of the yearly month-long fast and it is chiefly a time of thanksgiving. The other time is called the Festival of Sacrifice, which takes place at the same time as the pilgrimage to Mecca. Muslims worldwide commemorate on that occasion the supreme act of faith by Abraham when he offered to sacrifice his son in obedience to God and was rewarded by his son's deliverance.

In spite of the immense geographical scope of Islam, covering the whole world, and in spite of the fact that there is no central authority (person or council) for the faith, Islamic practice remains astonishingly uniform across the earth. This uniformity has to do with observance of the five "pillars" and traditional beliefs and practices handed down from the Prophet Muhammad. Otherwise Islamic life takes on the characteristics of the culture in which Muslims live. Many social attitudes and customs of dress, food, and behavior differ depending on whether Muslims live in, say, Egypt, Indonesia, Nigeria, or China. Some North American Muslims retain the ways of the lands from which they came, but others, in increasing numbers, have adopted American ways while staying faithful to the principles and practices of their faith. Muslims in North America have councils and associations to coordinate and facilitate activities, and they seek the wisdom of leaders to interpret aspects of their religious law. A lively Islamic press in the U.S. keeps its readers abreast of current social, political, and economic trends and suggests how they should react to them in the light of their faith.

The terrorist attacks against our country on September 11, 2001, had a double effect, one being to alienate great numbers of North Americans from Islam and Muslims. Because

Roxanne Dworak-El Filali, her daughter, Sakeena, 5, and husband, Mohammed El Filali join in a family portrait in their New Jersey home. The El Filalis, Moroccan Muslims, live upstairs in the same house as Roxanne's parents. Her father is a Ukranian Jew and her mother a Belgian Catholic who converted to Judaism. All are Americans.

they learned that the terrorists operated in the name of Islam, and because they are totally ignorant of that great civilization, they condemn Muslims as a whole. The other effect of September 11 has been to draw Muslims and other North Americans closer together. Again and again Islamic writers in newspapers and magazines have deplored senseless violence, sympathized with victims and survivors, and expressed solidarity with other Americans. They call for justice in international relations also, joining many Christians and others. An editorial in the August-September 2001 issue of *The Message International,* the organ of the Islamic Circle of North America, is entitled, "Should We Seek Justice or Revenge?" The author maintains that if the U.S. restrains itself from seeking revenge for the terrorist attacks, and instead seeks justice, then the trauma of the terrorist attacks can lead to a renewal of the human spirit in our nation and to a fresh dedication to justice in our relations with other peoples of the earth.

The one central divergence between Islam and Christianity is the understanding of Jesus Christ. All other differences are minor. On the one hand Christians may be gratified to learn that Jesus occupies a high place of honor in Islam. He is held as one of the prophets of the Almighty, and no calling of humankind is considered higher than that of prophet. According to Islam, Jesus was born of the Virgin Mary and lived a sinless life of sacrificial service to his people. When he was threatened by his enemies, God delivered him from a shameful death and exalted him to paradise. Many Muslims also believe that Jesus will return to earth at the end of the age. With all of this positive appreciation of Jesus, however, it is clear on the other hand that Jesus in Islam is not the same as Jesus Christ for the Christians. Muslims do not accept the title, Son of God, for Jesus, and they do not believe in the redemptive work of Christ upon the cross.

The Spiritual Life

Incline your hearts, O people of God, unto the counsels of your true, your incomparable Friend. The Word of God may be likened unto a sapling, whose root has been implanted in the hearts of men. It is incumbent upon you to foster its growth through the living waters of wisdom, of sanctified and holy words, so that its root may become firmly fixed and its branches may spread out as high as the heavens and beyond.

—Tablets of Baha'ullah

Building a Spiritual Civilization

The purpose of religion as revealed from the heaven of God's holy will is to establish unity and concord amongst the peoples of the world; make it not the cause of dissension and strife. The reign of God and His divine law are the most potent instruments and the surest of all means for the dawning of the light of unity amongst men. The progress of the world, the development of nations, the tranquility of peoples, and the peace of all who dwell on earth are among the principles and ordinances of God. Religion bestoweth upon man the most precious of all gifts, offereth the cup of prosperity, imparteth eternal life, and showereth imperishable benefits upon mankind.

—Tablets of Baha'ullah

Followers of the Baha'i faith live quietly in Hartford and its suburbs, 20 adults with their children. They are part of the five hundred believers in Connecticut who follow this world religion. Baha'i faith started in 19th century Iran, under the leadership of a Muslim named Mirza Husayn Ali Nuri, who became known as Baha'ullah (the glory of God). He was a charismatic figure claiming to be the latest in the long line of Manifestations of God that have been granted to humankind through the ages. These Manifestations, or Intermediaries, were necessary because otherwise God, of unknowable essence, would not be in any way accessible to humankind. Baha'ullah taught that the one true and living God covenanted with the created order not to leave it without guidance. All religions are expressions of this covenant, and their founders are Manifestations of the divine. Religion has the sole purpose of guiding human beings toward the unity for which they were created.

As can be imagined, this teaching, although couched in Islamic languages (Persian and Arabic) and coming from an Islamic setting, did not meet with Muslims' approval. The movement developed into a separate faith, becoming one of the most recent of world religions. Baha'ullah's following increased, not only in the Middle East, but also in South Asia and elsewhere. Today Baha'is number about five million worldwide. In 1894 the first community of Baha'is appeared in the U.S. Today Baha'is reside in about 7,000

North American localities and 1,700 local assemblies. They have built several schools and an imposing administration and worship center in Wilmette, Illinois.

The Baha'is in Hartford meet in their homes for worship and study. Their calendar is unique, based on a solar year, with 19 months of 19 days each. The day of worship is the first day of each of the 19 months. On that day they meet for a threefold purpose: devotional, administrative, and social. After prayers and readings from the sacred writings of Baha'ullah and others, they hear reports of Baha'i activities regional and worldwide and plan their communal life. Then the worshipers have a social time of fellowship together. Once a year they observe a month-long fast from food and drink as a spiritual exercise to draw near to God.

Ms. Ghita W. Blackmun, a Hartford member of the Baha'i community, spoke to me of the importance of languages in the Baha'i practices. Historically that religion has recommended the creation or the selection of an auxiliary language to facilitate the progress of humanity toward world unity. She pointed out that, although people once hoped that Esperanto, an artificially created language, would become the unifying world tongue, nowadays there is more hope for English or Spanish to fulfill that role. In the meantime, worship and study by Hartford area Baha'is are conducted in English, Spanish, and Persian, reflecting the multi-ethnic makeup of the participants.

Worship and all of life for Baha'is are centered on the single-minded focus of their beliefs in: the oneness of God, the oneness of humankind, and the oneness of religion. Baha'is believe that the world is gradually evolving toward a full realiza-

The Baha'i Temple in Wilmette, Illinois.

tion of essential unity, and as grateful followers of Baha'ullah's teaching, they seek to participate in the spiritual growth of the world by:

- Eliminating all kinds of prejudice.
- Promoting the equality of woman and man in all aspects of human society.
- Advocating the unity of truth, so that scientific and religious truths are in harmony.
- Working for compulsory education for all children throughout the world.
- Working for peace through world governance.
- Seeking to eliminate the extremes of wealth and poverty.
- Promoting free and independent investigation of truth by every individual.

(adapted from the official website of Baha'i faith)

Baha'is recognize that in spite of these high ideals for humanity, people can by their free will turn from what is best and permit their undisciplined physical passions to hinder their spiritual progress. But God is both just and merciful, ready to forgive those who turn from their misdeeds. As believers perfect their spiritual path by following the teachings of their founder and by works of

As with other faiths, Baha'i children learn by storytelling.

goodness, they prepare for the time of death where the soul will be separated from the body and will continue its course of spiritual perfection.

Baha'i faith has no clergy. The local assembly elects a nine-member administrative board to guide the community in its activities of teaching, publicity, worship, financial dealings, counseling, and so forth. The nine northeastern states have a regional council, and at the national level the administrative center in Wilmette, Illinois, supervises Baha'i ministries in the U.S. In Haifa, Israel, an imposing domed structure faced with Grecian-styled columns houses the Universal House of Justice, a nine-member council charged with the oversight of Baha'i communities in the whole world. Many people make pilgrimages to Haifa because it was near there that Baha'ullah died in 1892.

Baha'is have no special dietary restrictions, but they abstain from drugs and alcohol. They are free to take part in public life so long as they do not engage in partisan politics. They are required to obey the government in control and can take stands on moral and social issues. They believe, however, that political involvement would be a compromise of their primary emphasis, which is on the progress of human civilization toward unity.

Christians can go a long way toward agreeing with the Baha'is on their sober moral standards and high ideals for the future of the human race. Christian faith, however, humbly recognizes a tragic dimension to life which accounts for the desperate situation of individuals and peoples who are caught in the consequences of sin. And they believe that God became involved directly in the human predicament by sending Jesus, who by his death and Resurrection revealed both the enormous burden of sin and the magnificent scope of divine deliverance. To Christians it is not possible simply to assimilate this unique revelation into a framework of the unity of all religions, as the Baha'i faith does.

The World Soul

The supreme Self is neither born nor dies. He cannot be burned, moved, pierced, cut, nor dried. Beyond all attributes, the supreme Self is the eternal witness, ever pure, indivisible, and uncompounded, far beyond the senses and the ego. . . . He is omnipresent, beyond all thought, without action in the external world, without action in the internal world. Detached from the outer and the inner, this supreme Self purifies the impure.

—Atma Upanishad

We associate Hinduism with India, and rightly so, for the simplest description of Hinduism is that it is the principal religion of India, even though millions of people outside that land follow the Hindu way of life. Anyone who has read even a little about India is struck by the variety of cultures and languages that are found among its approximately 900 million people. And its main religion, Hinduism, measures up to the complex makeup of the population. Almost any aspect of the Hindu way of life that we describe can be contrasted with other aspects that are almost opposite. In addition, with Hinduism we enter a world strange to North American Christians: a world of many deities, of ornate temples dedicated to them, of births and rebirths, of colorful ceremonies, of deep philosophies, of a strict organization of social life, of disciplines of self-denial, and of an overall conviction that the world is sustained by a unifying force which cannot be described but that is present everywhere, a sort of world-soul. And to add to the strangeness of the Hindu way for us, its terms and practices are described in Sanskrit, the classical language of ancient India.

Hindus have moved out into most countries of the world, and they have come among us in the U.S., more that a million strong. About 23,000 call Connecticut their home, and there may be as many as 10,000 in the Greater Hartford area. An imposing temple stands in Middletown, Connecticut, a few miles from Hartford. It is the focal point of Hindu communal activities for the whole state. On Sunday afternoon, an average of some 2,000 devotees flock to the temple. However, they are not required to attend communal worship regularly. The practice is to observe daily devotional rites in the home, but on festival days or the special days of certain deities, many visit the temple. This large building houses offices, meeting rooms, classrooms, and, as the centerpiece, a group of 11 shrines. Each shrine is dedicated to a particular deity and contains richly ornamented images of the gods. In the center of the shrine area is a simulated Indian temple, with its elaborately carved, uplifting columns and figures, the whole bathed brilliantly in natural light from a soaring skylight. This gives the effect of an outdoor setting, as would commonly be the case in India.

Krithika Rajkumar, 9, left, and Novhi Vinod, 11, perform tradition-al Hindu dances at a workshop in Detroit, Michigan.

Worshipers come, having removed their shoes at the entrance, and go at will. Men and women mingle together freely. Many gather to stand reverently before the shrine of a particular god whose worship is the focus of the day. Several priests recite prayers and devotional texts. The people have brought gifts of fruit, rice, flowers, milk, and other things to the deity. After blessing the gifts, the priests walk among the people distributing bits of the food offerings to be eaten and also briefly placing a hat-like object made of silver upon the heads of the worshipers as a symbol of the protection offered by the deity whom they have invoked.

All the time that the greater number of people are gathered at one shrine, others go to the other images, bowing or prostrating themselves and offering gifts. A large bell hanging at the entrance to the worship area is rung by those who desire in that way to announce their presence and call upon the god of their choice.

Parents accompany their children to visit the shrines, and little ones run to and fro among the crowds. In the early afternoon there is a sudden hubbub as the older children are dismissed from Hindu Sunday school. Dozens of them scurry up to the worship area or go outside carrying their notebooks and study books. Adult education is also offered in various aspects of Hindu learning and in the Hindi language, the main language of India. One course is in Yoga, a term well known to North Americans who are not Hindus. Yoga is an ancient school of thought involving self-discipline by meditation, controlled breathing, and special postures.

What do the children learn about Hindu beliefs?

Their way of life is based on the teachings of ancient Scriptures that go back perhaps 3,000 years before Christ. These teachings were transmitted orally for centuries and then written down in the Sanskrit language. The writings include hymns to the gods of ancient Indians, as well as legends and prayers composed by unknown authors. Later collections of material, also accepted as authoritative Scripture, contain philosophical discourses, stories about the gods, epic poems, and devotional writings.

The sacred books tell about the indescribable essence, or world-soul, mentioned earlier, and the existence of thousands of deities, all of which are concerned with sustaining the world. Many Hindus say they do not worship a multitude of gods, but that the one supreme world-soul is manifested in a multitude of ways. So each image stands for one aspect of the supreme force of the universe. For example, there are gods of the sun, of marriage, of knowledge, of art and music, of fire, of agriculture, as well as gods who exemplify all the virtues of life required by the teachings of religion.

Life in this world is believed to be part of an eternal cycle of births and rebirths. What people do in the way of good or evil influences how they will be reborn after death, that is, their goodness may be rewarded with a higher level of existence or else they may be reduced to a lower level. The final goal however, lies beyond unending rebirths. All Hindus long for the eventual union of their soul with the world-soul, thereby breaking free from the cycle of births and rebirths. The good life, tending toward ultimate fulfillment, consists of moral behavior, service to others, seeking knowledge, worship, and devotion to one's personal deity who helps in the struggle with evil.

Reincarnation

As fruits and flowers will freely suit
the seasons,
The deed a man has done returns.
Respect and pride, gain, loss, growth and decay,
When life comes to its end, return
as once they were.
Pain by the self is wrought as well as joy,
The harvest of the past in rebirth you
shall taste.

—Mahabharata

Hindus observe a number of holy days and festivals honoring certain deities and celebrating the harvest and the new year. In Hartford, the press gives colorful coverage to these occasions, which include displays of traditional Indian dress and dancing. Also, families mark the significant moments of life with special rites, such as births, name-giving, first taking of solid food, head-shaving to remove symbolically the traces of evil from a previous life, ear-piercing, coming of age, marriage, and death.

This brief description of the Hindu way does not do justice to the extreme diversity in that religion. Little uniformity exists in the multitude of rituals, doctrines, devotions, art forms, and customs. Some adherents emphasize the ritual aspect of worship, others the devotional life of love for the gods, still others have little to do with the gods at all and concentrate on Hindu philosophy. And there are many whose religious practice is largely a matter of moral behavior. Hindus in general believe that no one religion is exclusively true, but that all genuine ways of faith are aspects of the one universal, all-encompassing truth.

Perhaps the one factor that unites most Hindus in our country is their vital link with India. And yet their lot is cast with the U.S. The drama of their lives as North American Hindus consists of working out their identity in this country, Gradually their religious beliefs and practices will adjust to the North American culture, which, in principle, supports and favors no one religion. What will this adjustment mean to devotees of the Indian deities? Dr. Shyamala Raman, a Hindu professor at St. Joseph College, West Hartford, spoke of one aspect of this adjustment. The Connecticut Hindus are organized in what is called the Connecticut Valley Hindu Temple Society, a type of organization that would have no reason for existence in India, given the traditional Hindu culture dominating that land. Such a society, of course, fits in with the North American religious scene where church-

Learning together at a Hindu school in northern India.

es operate through structures like districts and synods. Dr. Raman reacts against such an organization for North American Hindus, saying, "I pray privately, belonging to no organization, and when I participate in interfaith activities I represent only myself."

Christians differ from Hindus in a number of respects. First there is the historical importance of our faith: God created the world in the beginning and it will come to a meaningful end finally, contrary to the eternal cycles of existence in Hinduism. And then God is distinct from creation, not identified as the world-soul with all that exists. As distinct from creation, God endows humanity with personality and will to enter into a divine-human relationship. Contrary to the careful provisions in Hinduism for human betterment, overcoming evil by good works, enlightenment, and eventually reincarnation (rebirth), the Christian sees evil in tragic terms of moral rebellion against a personal God and a total incapacity to extricate oneself from the predicament of bondage to sin. So salvation comes from God alone who in a supreme act of love and grace, sent Christ to show the way of forgiveness and eventual victory over the last enemy, which is death.

Victory

Victory over thousands of external enemies in the battlefield is insignificant (it is of no avail) compared to the victory over one's inner enemies; vanquishing one's passions is an unparalleled conquest.

—Uttaraadhyayana Sutra

Prayer Offered During Annual Reflection on the Spiritual Journey

I forgive (without reservation) all living beings (who may have caused me any pain and suffering either in this life or previous lives), and I beg (again without reservation) for forgiveness from all living beings (no matter how small or large to whom I may have caused pain and suffering in this life or previous lives, knowingly or unknowingly, mentally, verbally, or physically, or if I have asked or encouraged someone else to carry out such activities). (Let all creatures know that) I have friendship with everyone and I feel no revenge (animosity or enmity) toward anyone.

—Prayer offered at time of Pratikraman

One of the holy places in the Hindu temple of Middletown, Connecticut, serves as a place of worship for the Jains of Connecticut. Although Jains number as many as 100,000 nationwide and have built more than 100 centers and temples, their number in Connecticut is not sufficient yet to make possible a separate temple for their use. With about 150 families in the state and well organized locally, they are part of the national organization called Jaina, which promotes unity and friendship among all Jains of North America.

The sanctum, or holy place, reserved for Jains in the Hindu temple reflects not only the relatively small size of the community in the state, but also the close affinity between the Jain religion and Hinduism. Jains revere as their founder a teacher, Lord Mahavira, who lived in Hindu India in the sixth century before Christ. This teacher was the last in a line of twenty-four great teachers whose times stretch back thousands of years into prehistory. Jains believe that these twenty-four individuals attained perfect knowledge and a degree of spiritual development that sets them apart from all other people. So they are venerated, and statues of two of them, the first and the last, have been placed in the sanctum in Middletown, Connecticut.

Mahavira taught his followers that they, too, can attain a state of perfect enlightenment if they follow the discipline that he set forth. Human beings find themselves in a universe that is eternal and uncreated. Destined to be born, to live, and to die, they are a part of the never-ending process of growth, development, death, and rebirth. At each stage of rebirth Jains may grow closer to perfection until they break free of the ongoing cycle of cause and effect, or the laws of nature. Then they achieve an indescribable state of perfect bliss. Readers will recognize in this belief a similarity to Hinduism, but Jains do not believe in god or gods. Theirs is a system in which the human being is capable alone of achieving a good life. To do this they must follow certain rules or principles. The first is nonviolence, and Jains consider it to be so important as to call it "the supreme religion." Nonviolence is extended to thought, words, and deeds, and involves the protection of the life of all living creatures. Jains, then, are strict vegetarians. Dr. Padam C. Jain, a psychiatrist in West Hartford, told me about his seven-year-old granddaughter, who was questioned by a journalist at the inauguration of the Jain sanctum in the Connecticut Hindu Temple. The reporter asked the little girl, "Do you eat meat?" She replied, "No, I am a vegetarian." Then he asked, "Why don't you eat meat?" And she said, "Because the animals are my friends."

For Jains nonviolence also includes restraining the consumption of earth's resources, abstaining from quarreling, fighting, criticizing, backbiting, and being dishonest in financial matters. Nonviolence in Jain practice is not, however, an absolute law. It is accepted that people must defend themselves in cases of aggression.

Other great principles of Jain morality are speaking the truth, sexual purity, abstaining from theft, and detachment from worldly possessions.

These principles were laid down for all adherents of the religion, men and women receiving equal status. There is no clergy in Jainism, but for those who go more deeply into the religion there exist orders of monks and nuns. These individuals pursue the life of righteousness with great strictness, even to the point of ascetic self-denial.

When Jains worship, they examine themselves, reflect on their progress in spiritual development, and contemplate the example of Mahavira. They pray in the sense of expressing their aspirations for a better life and voicing their regret for failure. The images of the teachers in the place of worship remind those who pray of the examples that are set before them of praiseworthy behavior. Also they are reminded of the great Jain principle of mutual dependence, or interdependence, whereby all living things are bound together for support. In everyday life, Jains often repeat the following act of obeisance in the Hindi language, called the Universal Prayer:

I bow to the ever-perfect victors.

I bow to the liberated souls.

I bow to the leaders of the Jain order.

I bow to the learned teachers.

I bow to the saints and sages everywhere in
   the world.

This five-fold obeisance erases all sins.

Amongst all that is auspicious, this is
   the foremost.

(Adapted from a souvenir booklet of the Jain Center of Greater Hartford)

Besides the visits to the sanctum in the Hindu temple, Hartford Jains also pray and meditate in their homes and meet in a study circle each month. Jain Scriptures, a vast literature of oral stories, poetry, biographies, and teachings, were gathered at various times in early history and finally codified and written down in definitive form about 450 years after Christ. Originally written in a Sanskrit dialect, they now exist in translation.

The Jain calendar is punctuated with several

festivals, two of them commemorating first the birth of Lord Mahavira, the revered teacher, and the other his achievement of release from the cycle of reincarnation. The third and most important festival is a time of reflection on one's spiritual and moral journey. Special recitations of holy texts are heard, fasting for eight days is observed, and people seek forgiveness from all whom they have offended during the previous year.

Although Jains do not number as one of the larger religions, being from four to six million worldwide, they are one of the oldest. They live mostly in India, and the languages and cultures of that land still mark the lives of Jains. They are known to be people with a strong social consciousness. In India they are noted for maintaining hospitals for aged and injured animals. Jains are not concerned about seeking converts to their way and show tolerance toward other religions, since one of their main teachings is the relative nature of truth, according to which any number of different viewpoints are possible depending on where, how, and when a particular belief is expressed.

Christians cannot but be deeply impressed by the moral seriousness of the Jain way. Some of its principal tenets need to be emphasized more in Christian circles. However, Christians do not believe that human beings are masters of their own destiny. They believe in God who created the universe and in whose hands is the destiny of all created things. Like Jains, Christians believe in the perfectibility of human beings, but for them development toward perfection takes place through a divine-human cooperation wherein the free human will, confessing its weakness, gratefully accepts the empowerment of God's Holy Spirit to grow in faith, hope, and holiness.

All Things Merge

Millions of sparks arise from a fire and, after existing separately, finally merge in it. Innumerable dust particles arise from the dust and will again become dust. Millions of waves arise on a large body of water, but the waves on water still remain water. The same way, from the infinite state, forms arise out of the formless and arising from it will all merge in it.

—Adi Granth

Meditation

Rise thou early and meditate on the Name. Yea, dwell on the Lord night and day; then thou sufferest not sorrow, and all thy woes depart.

—Adi Granth

Sikhs originally come from India, that area of the world which is an especially fruitful source of religious inspiration. But they are markedly different from other Indians in their way of life. In the region of the Punjab in the northwest a great teacher, called a guru, arose in the 15th century after Christ. His name is Guru Nanak, and after him came a series of nine other teachers following in his way and continuing until the early 18th century. The teachings of these ten teachers, plus writings of some Islamic and Hindu authors, were brought together into a large book of some 1,400 pages written in the Punjabi language of Northwest India. This collection of writings, in the form of poetry and hymns, constitutes the holy Scripture of Sikhism.

Two hundred and fifty thousand Sikhs have made their way to the U.S., and about 150 families of these live in Greater Hartford. Worldwide, Sikhs number about 22 million.

Hartford Sikhs go for weekly worship on Sunday at one of the two meeting places in the state. The gatherings for worship are centered around the holy Scriptures, which are displayed prominently in the room covered with a canopy. There is no ordained clergy, but designated leaders are in charge of the service. The order of worship is not rigidly fixed, but in general, worshipers gather, leaving their shoes at the door and covering their heads. First they bow reverently before the holy Scriptures that are on display. Then a hymn is sung from the holy book and accompanied by musical instruments. Men and women then sit separately to listen to readings or a talk on Sikh doctrine or history. Then the people stand for a prayer, which is also taken from the Scripture. The service ends with a hymn and the serving of a ceremonial food composed of semolina, sugar, and butter. Traditionally, the meeting places maintain kitchens for serving free food after the service to any who desire it. This meal is vegetarian, although Sikhs are not required to abstain from meat.

When I visited Mr. Amarjit Singh Buttar, a Sikh from Vernon, Connecticut, he took me to a room in his house which he had converted into a place for prayer. Simply furnished, it contained a copy of the Holy Scriptures covered with a canopy and a three-foot long ceremonial sword in its sheath, standing for the defense of the faith. Mr. Buttar told me that he begins and ends each day with devotions in the prayer room.

Sikh ceremonies are simple, unaccompanied by images or repetitive rites. This simplicity falls into line with their belief about God. The holy book refers to "One God, Eternal, Reality, The Name, Creator, All-pervading, Without fear, Without enmity, Unchanging, Unincarnate, Self-existent, (understood) through the Guru's [Teacher's] grace." So the teacher, Manak, and his successors were the ones who revealed this God to Sikhs. Along with the doctrine of one creator God, these ten great teachers also held to the view that life in this world is a continual round of births, deaths, and rebirths (reincarnations) until the soul achieves a state of purity in the eyes of God so that it is released to repose in the divine presence.

The Sikh religion has strict moral standards. Believers are held to a code of five virtues and five vices. The virtues are:

1. Truthfulness in living
2. Contentment
3. Patience
4. Faith in the great teacher, Nanak
5. Compassion.

The vices, whose description is necessary because of the human tendency to defy the moral law of humanity, are:

1. Lust
2. Anger
3. Greed
4. Excessive attachment to any earthly object or person
5. Pride.

Chicago area Sikhs celebrate Vaisakhi, a harvest festival, with a large parade featuring floats.

The Sikh shows evidence of unshorn hair, a sign of faith.

Sikhs put great emphasis upon humble service for the welfare of others, and are strongly opposed to any kind of discrimination, especially that which is based on social class or sex. In the U.S. they have suffered considerable discrimination themselves, mainly because of the distinctive dress of Sikh men. Traditionally they wear five signs of their faith:

- A short dagger symbolizing self-defense; this item may be worn in several sizes, even hung in miniature around the neck.
- Unshorn hair, a sign of faith.
- A comb in the hair to show cleanliness.
- A bracelet, binding one symbolically to the truth.
- A special undergarment symbolizing purity.

In addition men wear a turban, but, contrary to popular belief, it is not required by the religion. My friend, Mr. Buttar, told me that with their unusual dress Sikhs have had a difficult time fitting into U.S. society. He has occupied a responsible post in the Connecticut state government for 17 years, though, and he says that with patience and perseverance Sikhs can find acceptance.

The festival life of Sikhs is centered in the commemoration of events in the lives of the ten great teachers. Great moments in a person's life, such as birth and naming, marriage, initiation to special responsibility in the community, and death, are all marked by religious ceremonies.

Sikhs are organized with supervisory authority vested in the World Sikh Council. However, since most adherents still live in India where its historic sites are located, spiritual authority issues from Amritsar, India, the site of the most celebrated Sikh temple. Like others from Asia, the Sikhs in North America are going through the adaptation of their ways to a totally strange culture. Things like language, customs, and dress are gradually changing as the Sikhs make a place for themselves here.

Much of what Sikhs believe about God is similar to Christians' beliefs. Both confess God as Creator, sustainer of the universe, and one intimately involved in the events of the world and the lives of human beings. Both faiths believe that divine help is available for those who seek deliverance from the power of evil. Sikhs turn to their teacher, or guru, Nanak, for the revelation of what God is like, whereas Christians find in Jesus Christ, the perfect revelation of God; not only in his teachings but also in his very being, as the Son of God, showing forth to the world the loving, redeeming, empowering nature of the Almighty. Both faiths put great emphasis on a personal relationship between the believer and God.

Lovingkindness

As a mother at the risk of her life watches over her own child, her only child, so let every one cultivate a boundless (friendly) mind toward all beings. And let him cultivate good will towards all the world, a boundless (friendly) mind, above and below and across, unobstructed, without hatred, without enmity.

—Sutra Nipata

Craving

When a person lives heedlessly, his craving grows like a creeping vine. He runs now here and now there, as if looking for fruit, a monkey in the forest. If this sticky, uncouth craving overcomes you in the world, your sorrows grow like wild grass after rain. If, in the world, you overcome the uncouth craving, hard to escape, sorrows roll off you, like water beads off a lotus.

—Dhammapada

One of the Buddhist groups in suburban Hartford has converted a former school of gymnastics into a center for its activities. The abbot, or spiritual director, said wryly, "Our building used to be a place for physical exercise. Now it is a place for spiritual exercise." When you remove your shoes and go inside you are introduced into an exotic, Far Eastern setting. The large, carpet-covered floor is bare except for round cushions on which participants in the ceremonies are invited to sit. At one end of the room the wall is lined with statues, a large one of the Buddha in the center, with several smaller ones on either side. Gongs, drums, and splendid examples of oriental art complete the furnishings.

Who is or was the Buddha? His name was Siddhartha Gautama, and the term "Buddha" is a title of honor, meaning "Enlightened One." He lived 600 years before Christ in India, so his thought world was like that of the Hindus, at least at first: a universe in which human beings are caught up in an endless cycle of births, deaths, and rebirths, endless, that is, until they achieve enlightenment and release from the world of suffering. But the Buddha was an original thinker, a genius of spiritual psychology, and his teachings diverged from Hinduism. He saw human beings as free moral agents, autonomous in their ability to work out their own destiny by adhering to certain principles. That destiny is understood as achieving "Buddhahood," that is, the enlightenment of the great teacher, by devotion, self-discipline, and the practice of compassion. The Buddha was silent on the subject of God, and Buddhists consider whatever energy there is behind the existence of the universe as nameless. So when Buddhists gather in their meeting place they do not worship in the sense of praying to a god to ask for divine help. Their spiritual exercises include the following, practiced at different times and on different occasions, and depending on the branch of the religion to which they belong:

The Three Refuges, accompanied by three bows—

I seek refuge in the Enlightened One (Buddha).

I seek refuge in the true teaching.

I seek refuge in the community.

The Four Noble Truths, in which instruction is given—

the truth of suffering, both physical and mental, which is the basic fact of life;

the truth of the cause of suffering, which is desire; whatever one desires and cannot obtain causes pain and suffering;

the truth of the cessation of suffering, which will come about when a person gives up all desire and craving;

the truth of the path to the ending of suffering, by means of the *Noble Eightfold Path—*

right belief,

right thought,

right speech,

right action,

right livelihood,

right effort,

right mindfulness,

right meditation.

The Five Precepts, ceremonially read, which summarize Buddhist moral standards, in which followers undertake to abstain from—

taking the life of any living being;

taking anything that is not given;

sexual misconduct and other forms of overindulgence;

bad speech;

taking intoxicants.

Burning of incense to the Buddha in appreciation.

Chanting of words from the teaching.

Prayers and offerings to the Buddha and to revered exemplary figures from ancient times; these prayers may be understood as aspirations of the devotees as they place themselves in the light of the objects of their devotion.

Disciplined meditation in both a seated position and walking.

The Buddhists who gather in the converted gym in Greater Hartford are basically of Vietnamese origin, although many native North Americans of European and other ethnicities participate in the activities, either as inquirers or as converts to the Buddhist way. About eight other centers exist in the Hartford area, each one representing a particular branch such as Japanese, Tibetan, or Chinese. Buddhism broke out of the Indian setting early in its history and developed with great vitality in other Asian countries. It came to the U.S. in the 19th century and has grown to a solid institutional presence with more than 1,000 centers and perhaps 2½ million adherents. Exact figures are not possible because of the large number of inquirers and converts, many of whom maintain membership in other religious bodies along with Buddhism. The highly developed discipline of meditation among followers of the Buddha has attracted thousands to take up that religion. Numerous monasteries for monks and nuns in the U.S. have outreach activities into neighboring communities, educational institutions, and charitable organizations, all taking inspiration from the Buddha.

Buddhism is truly international, with about 400 million adherents worldwide, but with its thor-

This reclining Buddha is in a Buddha park in Laos.

oughly pluralistic makeup as a religion, it still maintains close ties with its Asian origins. In Hartford, some ceremonies are conducted in the Vietnamese language, others in Tibetan. I was shown a collection of the Chinese translations of holy texts from the original Sanskrit and Pali tongues of India. Young North American converts sometimes take up the study of Tibetan or other Asian languages of Buddhism. The translation of holy texts into English remains an unfinished task.

But withal Buddhism holds a universal attraction for its rational approach to life coupled with its motivation to seek wisdom in a world understood to be composed of unreal, impermanent phenomena, a wisdom that eventually leads to release from suffering and awareness of the true nature of all things.

Like any religion Buddhism provides abundant opportunities for its adherents to celebrate festivals, rites, and ceremonies having to do with everyday life. The festivals are observed according to a lunar calendar, and they especially note events in the Buddha's life and developments in the early history of the religion. Details vary greatly according to the country or culture in which Buddhism is practiced. In fact, details on all aspects of devotion, doctrine, and philosophy vary so much from one part of the world to another that a short sketch such as this does not do justice to the complexity of world Buddhism.

With regard to meditation and its undeniable benefits to people who are harried and distracted by our hyperstimulated generation with its frenetic craving for "things," many people, especially Protestants, do not realize that in the Christian tradition there exists abundant teaching on meditation as a discipline of life. So they do not have to go elsewhere if they feel the need for instruction in how to meditate. On the other hand quite a few Christians have delved into Buddhist methods of meditation without leaving their churches and have been strengthened in their Christian experience.

God, to whom witness is borne in the Bible, is totally different from anything in Buddhism. The biblical God is a personal, ever-present deity, willing to enter into communication with human beings, and yet is also the Creator and sustainer of the universe. Likewise the story of God's dealings with humanity, having a beginning at creation, and an end at the return of Christ, calls for a linear view of time that contrasts sharply with the endless cycles of time in Buddhism.

Both Christians and Buddhists share a deep concern for suffering as a basic element in life (*the* basic element in Buddhism), although the way to deal with suffering is not the same in the two perspectives. The goal of Buddhism is the elimination of suffering by suppressing its cause, desire. Christians, on the other hand, see suffering, even with all its negative qualities, to be the setting for God's redemptive purpose as Christ became historically the willing sufferer for all of humankind: "For Christ also suffered for sins once for all, the righteous for the unrighteous, in order to bring us to God" (I Peter 3:18a). In conversation with Buddhist friends, Christians may discover other points of agreement and disagreement on the subject of suffering.

These young men are studying to be Buddhist monks in Laos.

Song of the Sky Loom

> Oh our Mother the Earth, oh our Father the Sky,
> Your children are we, and with tired backs
> We bring you the gifts that you love.
> Then weave for us a garment of brightness;
> May the warp be the white light of morning,
> May the weft be the red light of evening,
> May the fringes be the falling rain,
> May the border be the standing rainbow.
> Thus weave for us a garment of brightness
> That we may walk fittingly where birds sing,
> That we walk fittingly where grass is green,
> Oh our Mother the Earth, oh our Father the Sky!

—Tewa Song

From Wakan Tanka, the Great Spirit, there came a great unifying life force that flowed in and through all things—the flowers of the plains, flowing winds, rocks, trees, birds, animals—and was the same force that had been breathed into the first man. Thus all things were kindred, and were brought together by the same Mystery.

—Luther Standing Bear (Oglala)

There were many religions in America long before Christianity, or any of the others discussed here, arrived on the scene. The religions of the Native American Indians were original to this country, or at least for as far back as we can go, even into prehistory. All other religions are "imports." This is reason enough to include the truly native faiths in our discussion, even though they are not represented in the religious communities to be found in the Hartford area. There are several tribes living in the state of Connecticut, however, and I have had the privilege of meeting a few individuals from among them. Because of the extreme importance of the presence of these and other Native Americans, their religions are included, even if briefly. Certain unusual difficulties stand in the way of dealing with them:

1. Native American religions are many, even several hundred, in number, and any attempt to describe them as a whole is bound to distort their reality.

2. The greatest difficulty in talking about these religions seems to me to be the historical burden that weighs heavily upon the Native Americans and others alike. Those who prac-

Native American children sing at First United Methodist Church, Norman, Oklahoma.

tribal identity, the close interaction between humans and nature, the unity of the spiritual with the material, and the use of native languages.

For quite a few years now there has been underway throughout the country a revival of native religious practice and an effort to affirm the Native American heritage from the times before the European invasion. Supporting this revival is the American Indian Religious Freedom Act of 1978, which made it the official "policy of the United States to protect and preserve for American Indians their inherent right of freedom to believe, express, and exercise the traditional religion of the American Indian, Eskimo, Aleut and Native Hawaiians, including but not limited to access to sites, use and possession of sacred objects, and the freedom to worship through ceremonials and traditional rites." (See U.S. Code, Title 42, Section 1996.)

3. Up to now non-Native Americans have had little opportunity or inclination to learn about the spiritual nature of Native American faith. There exists a certain curiosity regarding the distinctive dress, dances, ceremonies, and customs of the indigenous populations, but this is counterbalanced by the historical disregard that North Americans have shown for Native American beliefs. In the name of Christian civilization, the early European settlers despised Native American religions, considering them as pagan cults. When the tribes were subjugated and the intruders ran the schools, children were forbidden to speak their own languages and practice their religions. However, encouraging signs are appearing, indicating that people are showing

tice these faiths are doing so from the terrible position of being not quite themselves at all. For the last 300 years, they have been deprived of their lands, uprooted, in some cases almost destroyed by our forebears who came to settle this land. Consider the lot of the Seminoles, forced to leave their homes in Florida and resettle in distant Oklahoma. Think of the Cherokees who also were exiled from their homeland to the West. And even those tribes who were not moved en masse were so battered and oppressed that they almost lost their identity. In many cases some of the precious things of their culture were suppressed, such as the attachment to ancestral lands, the strong ties of more respect for and interest in the traditions of the earliest Americans. For example, United Methodists have had on their church calendar since 1988 the special observance called Native American Awareness Sunday, which highlights the culture and achievements of Native Americans.

4. Finally, the historical burden is compounded and complicated by the fact that thousands of Native Americans have been Christianized. It is enough to confound and shame a non-Native American, to think that on the one hand, schools and churches, Christian in name, were used to crush and suppress the spiritual expression of the first Americans. But, then, on the other hand, many of the subjugated accepted Christianity, and taking inspiration from the example of Christ, they have become faithful followers of the gospel, returning good for evil. We outsiders have only vague ideas of what takes place in the experience of Christian Native Americans. One thing seems fairly evident. They do not give up their traditional beliefs, but work out some synthesis of those ways with Christian truth. The manner in which this is done must vary greatly from tribe to tribe and from person to person. The Right Reverend Carol Gallagher, a bishop of the Episcopal Church and a member of the Cherokee nation, put it this way: "[F]or me all of my spiritual and cultural tradition is my Old Testament." (*The Witness* [April 2002]: 25.) I understand this to mean that the religion of her tribe was used by God to prepare her for the Word of the gospel. Then another Native American, Chief Hockeo Roy Sebastian of the Eastern Pequots of Connecticut, and a lay leader in The United Methodist Church, said that he lives in two worlds at the same time and is blessed in each. These two testimonies hint at the complex working of mind and spirit when Native American spirituality and the Word of Christ interact. We had better leave it with the Holy Spirit (or Great Spirit, as the native people say) and humbly acknowledge that these religions remain to be discovered by outsiders. But one may hope that in friendly interactions with those of a particular Native American nation, we may be able to discover something of the reality of at least one tradition.

THE SPIRITUAL LIFE

Incline your hearts, O people of God, unto the counsels of your true, your incomparable Friend. The Word of God may be likened unto a sapling, whose root has been implanted in the hearts of men. It is incumbent upon you to foster its growth through the living waters of wisdom, of sanctified and holy words, so that its root may become firmly fixed and its branches may spread out as high as the heavens and beyond.

—Tablets of Baha'ullah

Baha'ism

2

WHY INTERFAITH COMMUNITY?

Religious communities have lived apart for so long, especially in the United States, that we cannot take the value and importance of interfaith community for granted. Some may even object to the idea of bringing people of different religions together, fearing that it would make for confusion, theological compromise, or a weakening of the bonds that keep members of a particular church together. These objections and others will be answered in chapter 3 when we look into the resources of Christian faith for interreligious activity. As a Christian writing for Christians, I have some reasons to justify efforts at interfaith community. Those of other faiths will have their reasons, too, similar or not to the ones offered here. Thus there surfaces already a reason for us to get together with people of other beliefs: that is, to compare and coordinate our particular purposes for trying to create community. Here are some reasons that seem important to me.

In our land we have many religions, but they are all relatively small groups compared to Christianity, the majority faith. These minority communities, representing one or two percent, say, of our total population, or less, live terribly vulnerable lives in a land where little or no interfaith community exists. The Federal Bureau of Investigation has reported that in the year 2000 there were 1,472 incidents of religious hate crimes in the U.S. In the aftermath of the terrorist attacks on September 11, 2001, a rash of such violent acts took place as people gave vent to their anger by attacking individuals and properties of other religions, especially Islam. Virulent verbal attacks continue to occur, like the recent well-publicized statements by a famous Christian television preacher that Islam is a religion of violence that aims at world domination. Such events are evidence of what happens when there is no interfaith community. And compared with other countries, our land has a relatively small percentage of people belonging to other faiths than Christianity. What about countries of the world that have millions of citizens divided into rival religious communities? Recent years have witnessed the most horrible outbreaks of violent destruction of life and property in interreligious conflict. We may think that our nation would never be the scene of religious mayhem, like incidents that have occurred in the former Yugoslavia, Indonesia, India, Nigeria, and elsewhere. But as long as interfaith community is neglected, the seeds of more serious antagonism between faiths are there waiting to bear fruit in the poisoned soil of indifference, ignorance, and ill will.

Religion is one of the most fruitful areas in which leaders can exploit prejudices, making false claims and promises to achieve power or to further political ambitions. The most striking example in our time is that of Osama bin Laden, whose demagogic powers have incited multitudes of Muslims against other religions. And in our land, leaders use the mass media to spread distorted information about other faiths supposedly to rally Christians against attacks upon their beliefs and institutions. One fears, however, that negative harangues of this kind serve mainly to enhance the power of the speakers over their hearers. To counteract religious antagonism and the ever-present danger of interreligious violent conflict is reason enough to create interfaith community.

WE NEED EACH OTHER

Do we really think that we can go it alone in the world? The whole thrust of our civilization says no. Witness the United Nations, globalization, international trade agreements, intercontinental communication and the world wide web. When we say that we need each other, we are talking about people with whom God has given us the grace to live in this world. Because we are all in the same general human situation in which we depend on each other more and more, the ties that bind us together need to be strengthened. The late Dr. Frederick Streng, professor of religious studies at Southern Methodist University, Dallas, Texas, spoke about this mutual interdependence:

[W]e may… sense the relevance for every Christian, as well as for every person on earth, to understand and cooperate with others to solve issues that affect all of us on this planet. Through communications technology and political-economic interdependencies, all human beings are neighbors. By understanding others, we may not only be able to avoid unnecessary conflict and destruction, but even help each other to achieve a more abundant life." ("The Challenge of Religious Pluralism to Christian Theology and the Church," Newsletter of the Office on Christian-Muslim Relations of the National Council of Churches, U.S.A., [October 1986])

But religion, some may say—that is different: "Our faith is completely sufficient. We do not need the contribution of other faiths to make our life more satisfactory." But we are not talking about one religion needing another religion. Our concern is people who find themselves in a common "package" of interdependent humanity. And in our respective ways faith is a primary element of our identity, even as we saw in Chapter 1. Therefore, as we mutually count on each other in all aspects of life, we can be sure that faith enters into the picture.

Learning about Being Mutual Witnesses

For one thing, we need each other to learn about being mutual witnesses to our faiths. Christians have always felt the desire to witness to others about the love of God as revealed in Christ. We have drawn inspiration from the example of the early followers of Christ, who, filled with the joy of their faith, exclaimed, "we cannot keep from speaking about what we have seen and heard" (Acts 4:20). But we have not always realized that believers in other religions also feel a desire to witness. We have often considered those to whom we witness as simply representatives of a rival religion, not recognizing in them something of the same eagerness to share a faith that we Christians feel. When I say, "eagerness to share a faith," I do not mean missionary motivation in the commonly understood meaning of the word "mission," even though some religions, such as Islam and Buddhism, teach their followers to reach out for converts. In a broader sense, people of all faiths find satisfaction and fulfillment in their holy Scriptures, their worship, their ideals, and their communal life. And they like for others to know about what they experience.

As interfaith community is created, as the flow of friendly, mutually meaningful discourse takes place between us, we will discover ways in which other people communicate their beliefs. The ways they do this, sometimes surprising and often beautiful, will help us Christians deepen our own lives of witness. This communication will also make possible a rich community of loyal testimony, in which we sense the satisfaction of faithfulness to our Christian convictions and at the same time grant generous respect to mutual witnesses in other traditions. Lest this suggestion sound strange and even unreal, we hasten to add that as Christians we cannot be content with a kind of stalemate of mutual witness. Learning to be respectful yet forthright in our faith-sharing may lead to a situation of spiritual expectancy, in which God the Holy Spirit is free to work for the good of all concerned.

Seeing Ourselves as Others See Us

We need each other to serve as a moral check on our respective communities. Although we may feel that our moral standards as Christians are perfectly adequate, we cannot see ourselves as others see us. We may not realize how in some ways we do not live up to our ethical ideals. We need comment and criticism from outside, as does every faith group. A moral lethargy may come upon a people who will not accept criticism. Unfortunately, religious groups have too often hurled accusations of unethical behavior at each other, each one assuming a position of superiority toward the others.

Examples of this practice can be found in the history of Muslim-Christian relations. Christians have accused Muslims of gross sensuality because of their institution of polygamy. Muslims, in turn, have pointed out that polygamy as a stable, social practice is preferable to prostitution and other kinds of extramarital involvements that are common in the lands where Christians are in the majority. Also, Christians often accuse Muslim peoples of being turbulent and warlike, unable to settle their differences among themselves. Muslims point out that Christian countries fought two world wars in the first half of the 20th century. Such mutual recrimination serves no good purpose. In fact, for every moral defect in one community, a corresponding defect in the other community can usually be found. On the other hand, as interfaith community develops, the different partners can learn from each other how better to obey the moral imperatives of their faith, and on occasion they may point out respectfully and humbly certain ethical failings in one or another group.

Secularism Is Friend and Foe

Again we need each other to form a united defense against the degrading influences of secularism. This point requires some clarification because we in the U.S. have long been grateful for the secular nature of our Republic. It makes sure that no one religion or church is given power and authority over the others. The separation of church and state is a basic feature of our national life. So secularism, a policy whereby religion is deprived of official status or influence, can be appreciated for providing an atmosphere of freedom and equality for all religions. Secularism may be the only way by which a truly pluralistic society can thrive.

I call attention, however, to the fact that secularism, in the name of being religiously neutral, actually interjects into our life an alternate choice, a rival ideology, that works against religious faith. Most of the time the secular government is harmless enough. It is even beneficial, helping regulate all kinds of activities, managing, supervising, and providing services for the people. But world history has furnished several examples of how other countries, such as Italy under the Fascists, Germany under the Nazis, and the Soviet Union under Communism, developed secular ideologies of the state that demanded the absolute loyalty of their citizens, regardless of the consequences. That is the threat of a secular state. In such a situation, the government deceives people into thinking that their concerns and the secular concerns of the state are identical. Religion is manipulated to serve secular ideological purposes.

We can see hints of this in America. The secular ideology of American nationalism is alive among us. We do not usually call it that. It is called "following the American dream," or "love of freedom," or "defending democracy," or simply "patriotism." Other forces have an even more subtle secular influence upon our lives, such as financial affluence, materialism, television culture, and the built-in dominance of one race or class. This is what I mean by the degrading influences of secularism, which all religious people must resist. Interfaith community can help bring like-minded believers of various communities to an awareness of its danger.

Setting an Example for Peace

We need each other so that we can speak with a united voice for peace in the world. Here we note the favored place that we have in the U.S., a truly pluralistic society. We have equal opportunities, as religious people, to speak out for world peace. Each of our faiths has its blueprint for a peaceful society; and, besides similarities, each one has a theological or social distinctiveness. But as interfaith community is developed, we can blend our ideas, learning how they complement each other. Morever, some of us can tone down our expectations for dominating the world. We can see ourselves as beleaguered people of faith, faced with the massive forces of irreligion worldwide.

Religious gatherings and leaders often issue statements about world peace. There is nothing wrong with such statements, but they are singularly ineffective in stopping wars. I doubt if the big power magnates in the world are going to let little bishops, priests, rabbis, or ulama stand in their way of doing what they want. So, rather than formulating more statements, it would probably be better to show by our example, in particular situations, how people can live together in interreligious peace.

Working Together on Social Issues

Finally, we need each other for insight into solving our social problems. As people of faith in community, we might have more success working at these issues than on the global matter of world peace. And as we strive together to heal the social ills of our people, we will be indirectly contributing to world peace. I am thinking of crying social needs such as relations between labor and management, immigration, population control, legal protection for the poor, care of the handicapped, drugs and alcohol, protection of the environment, health care, and criminal justice.

INTERFAITH COMMUNITY ENHANCES CHRISTIAN SELF-UNDERSTANDING

Through interfaith community we can deepen our understanding of our own faith, seen in the light of other faiths. All through history, Christians have drawn upon other religions and philosophies to help them interpret Christian faith for themselves and for others. In the New Testament we find many examples of this practice, and it continues to the present. In a United Methodist newspaper, a writer quoted the ancient Greek philosopher, Plato, to support his interpretation of the church's ethical responsibility in a particular case of injustice. (*United Methodist Review* [March 15, 2002]) Beverly Reddick, missionary-in-residence at the General Board of Global Ministries of The United Methodist Church, testified how the writings of Buddhist peace activist Thich Nhat Hanh have helped her in dealing with strong emotions in her personal life that, unchecked, lead to violent thoughts, language, and actions. ("Mission Matters," [June 2002], General Board of Global Ministries)

So today, we have the privilege and opportunity of not only drawing upon ancient, not explicitly Christian, wisdom, but of joining in community with men and women of faith traditions going back thousands of years and listening to them. If we listen humbly, it is likely that our Christian faith will be deepened and enriched. Values such as respect for the environment, the nurture of our inner being through meditation, the discipline of fasting, the spiritual meaning of God's oneness and its influence upon the wholeness of human life—these and numerous others are expounded and lived out with astonishing clarity and depth in the various religious communities with which we have to do.

The Dalai Lama, leader of Tibetan Buddhism worldwide, expressed from the Buddhist viewpoint thoughts that can be echoed by Christians as they seek better self-understanding in interfaith community. He wrote in 1997: "I believe it is extremely important that we extend our understanding of each other's spiritual practices and traditions. This is not necessarily done in order to adopt them ourselves, but to increase our opportunities for mutual respect. Sometimes, too, we encounter something in another tradition that helps us better appreciate something in our own." (Donald W. Mitchell and James A. Wiseman, eds. *The Gethsemani Encounter: Dialogue on the Spiritual Life by Buddhist and Christian Monastics* [New York: Continuum, 1997], p. x) Of course we will also encounter things with which we do not agree, and that is another question. In the next chapter, we will read about what to do when we disagree in interfaith community.

To Be Faithful to the Christian Mission in the World

The document "Partnership in God's Mission" clearly states the theology of mission of The United Methodist Church. Here are some pertinent lines from that declaration: "The church experiences God's mission as it pours itself out for others, crossing all boundaries to identify with the struggles and needs, the yearnings and sorrows, the joys and fears, the confusion and doubt, and the quest for true human dignity among all people everywhere...."

Where, in this comprehensive mandate, does interfaith community find a place? The statement says further: "Mission in a new age will increasingly encounter persons of other religious faiths. Many religions of the world are experiencing a resurgence of influence and fervor. Engagement and encounter, conversation and cooperation with persons of other religious faiths provide a unique opportunity for complete and enriching Christian witness." ("Partnership in God's Mission," General Board of Global Ministries, 1986)

Seeking to create interfaith community means crossing boundaries between religions, identifying with the hopes, joys, and fears of other religious communities, and also with their histories and achievements. It means humbly joining believers from many ways of faith to face the burden and the mystery of life and death and to work for righteousness inspired by the hope that we have in Jesus Christ, through the love that God has so freely bestowed upon us.

Some years ago, church leaders from many nations gathered in Thailand to talk about what at that time was a fairly new endeavor for Christians, the aspect of mission called "interfaith dialogue." They issued a statement which included the following:

We see dialogue…as a fundamental part of our Christian service within community. In dialogue we actively respond to the command to "love God and your neighbor as yourself." As an expression of our love, our engagement in dialogue testifies to the love we have experienced in Christ. It is our joyful affirmation of life against chaos, and our participation with all who are allies of life seeking the provisional goals of a better human community. (Chiang Mai Theological Consultation on Dialogue in Community, World Council of Churches, *Ecumenical Review* 29 [July 1977]: 261)

This linking of interfaith dialogue (or as we would say, "interfaith community") with love of one's neighbor reminds us of the characteristic way in which the founder of Methodism, John

Wesley, linked the love of our neighbor with the love of God. Wesley lived many years before the time of interfaith dialogue. He was not able to benefit from the first-hand knowledge of other religions that later exploration, historical studies, and communication made possible. But he was truly a spiritual leader for the future. We of this present time resonate with his resounding emphasis on the universal love of God for all the world and the Christian response to that love in faith that leads to loving deeds in behalf of all people. Mission in this sense might be understood as "sharing love." In a sermon on I Corinthians 13, Wesley wrote, "I am thoroughly persuaded that what St. Paul is here directly speaking of is the love of our neighbour…. And this love sweetly constrains him [the Christian] to love every child of man with the love which is here spoken of…a love of benevolence—of tender good-will to all the souls that God has made. (*The Sermons of John Wesley*, 1872 ed. [Nampa, Idaho: Wesley Center for Applied Theology, Northwest Nazarene University], available through http://wesley.nnu.edu/sermons)

It is obvious that Christian mission as expressed in interfaith community does not involve either direct proclamation of the gospel or the seeking of converts from other faiths to Christianity. However, it is no less a part of mission. Other aspects of the Christian sharing of love likewise do not involve direct proclamation or the seeking of converts. One thinks of medical ministries, the service of Christian engineers, technicians, agricultural experts, and so on. The Christian outreach of love includes the whole person of those who bear witness—their deeds, words, and attitudes. And we believe that it is the Holy Spirit who validates, integrates, and perfects the varied aspects of Christian witness, working out in God's ways the full purposes of divine love.

The purpose of this book is to suggest ways in which we can create interfaith community and be perfectly loyal to the Christian mission as understood in its broad and many-faceted nature. For us Christians interfaith community *is* mission, and that is reason enough to create it.

THE FINAL GOAL IS WORTH THE EFFORT

Along with the foregoing reasons for creating interfaith community, there stands, from the Christian perspective, a magnificent final goal for such activity. Each participant will formulate a particular goal depending on the tradition represented. For Christians, the whole enterprise is based upon their conviction that life at its best consists of uninterrupted communication between God and human beings, a communication made possible by the coming of Jesus Christ into the world. And one result of the divine-human interaction is that Christians are constrained to imitate God's action and seek free and meaningful interaction with other people, not only of their own faith, but also of other faiths. If the communication is free, then we believe the future prospects are open. Neither we nor the others who join in interfaith community are fixed, unchangeable types. We are children of a hopeful future. Unknown though that future is, we can set as our goal the glory of the God of the future: that our interfaith efforts might reflect the surpassing excellence of the One who has inspired us to undertake them.

VICTORY

Victory over thousands of external enemies in the battlefield is insignificant (it is of no avail) compared to the victory over one's inner enemies; vanquishing one's passions is an unparalleled conquest.

—*Uttaraadhyayana Sutra*

Jainism

3

RESOURCES OF CHRISTIAN FAITH

Among the resources of Christian faith which help us to create interfaith community, the basic undergirding comes from the assurance of faith. After considering this assurance, the chapter examines various attempts by Christians to find a place for other religions in the divine ordering of the world. The next topic deals with how a faithful Christian witness fits into interfaith community. This question of witness leads to the demanding question of how we face rival truth claims by other religions. Finally, the chapter suggests some ways to deal with differences between Christianity and other religions.

Creating interfaith community demands a strong Christian commitment. If would-be participants are unsure of their faith, they may easily become confused and take a wrong course as they mingle with people of other faiths. Insecure Christians may feel threatened by the claims and contrary beliefs of others. And feeling threatened in their own identity, they may erect and draw back behind walls of false security, from which they attack the adherents of other religions, accusing them of false doctrines and practices and holding up Christian beliefs and practices as superior. Such a reaction goes against interfaith community.

I heard of a young seminary student who took a course on Islam. She complained in a letter to her parents that the professor was trying to make Muslims out of the Christians in the class. I knew the professor well, and he was a stalwart and faithful Christian. He was trying to teach about Islam in as friendly and understanding a way as is possible for one who is a non-Muslim. The student felt threatened by the sympathetic approach, so she reacted by defending herself against an imagined effort to proselytize.

Insecure Christians may also react to other faiths in a different way. They may be tempted to give up their Christian identity and join the ranks of another religious group. Numerous cases of Christians' changing their religion may be understood as a movement from an insecure, uncommitted Christian status to security and stability in another religious identity.

Often, too, ungrounded Christians, when exposed to other ways of belief, are tempted not to be converted but in their uncertainty to assume that all religions are essentially the same and that there is no need to take a decisive, firm stand for the uniqueness of Christianity. To be fair, we cannot say that all Christians who follow this line of thinking are wavering, insecure believers. It is just that somehow they reach their conclusions by a process of reasoning which makes Christianity simply one among a multitude of faiths.

Interfaith community is not a desirable option for those Christians who are not sure of their commitment and convictions. It is not for searchers after an anchor for their souls. Interfaith community is for Christians who have drawn deeply from the resources of their faith, who have without reserve committed their lives to Jesus Christ, the way, the truth, and the life (John 14:6).

CHRISTIAN VIEWS OF OTHER RELIGIONS

A Christian firmly grounded in the faith is not exempt from wrestling with the perplexing question of how to regard other religions from a theological point of view. Christians of all persuasions have proposed a variety of answers to this question. I have made a list of some of the most common answers. Give yourself a test to see if you agree or disagree with these answers.

Differing Views

1. It is impossible for us to say that all religions are fundamentally alike or of equal value, simply because we know only one, and can know only one, that is, Christianity. Our grasp of other religions must remain that of an outsider.

2. Believers in other religions are lost in their attachment to a false religion. Their only hope is to be converted to Christianity.

3. Christians and people of other religions should cooperate because they have much to learn from each other.

4. Believers in all religions are going to the same place anyway, so why all the concern over the differences between our religions?

5. Believers in other religions are seeking God, but they will find the fulfillment of their search only in Christianity.

6. God may have truly spoken through other channels than the Christian revelation, but we cannot be absolutely sure, since our only channel to divine truth is through Christ.

7. All religions, including Christianity, are produced by human beings, so they are mixtures of truth and error. Only God is wholly true.

8. In other religions, men and women are addressing God. The initiative is wholly human. In the Christian faith, and in the Bible, God is addressing humankind.

9. Christians should seek, in their relationships with people of other faiths, to purify their religions without condemning them, and thus to reveal to them the Christ who is hidden within their religions.

10. The only way we can identify the truth and goodness of what believers in other religions think and do is in the light of God's revelation through Christ.

11. Other believers, in the best expression of their faith, are really seeking to follow Christ, without even realizing it.

You will no doubt find some of these answers partly true and partly false, others clearly wrong, and still others probably true. The list may be summarized as follows:

a. Other religions are merely human creations, even expressions of rebellion against God, and so should be considered as opposed to Christianity.

b. Christianity and other religions are basically the same. Their differences are due to historical, social, and cultural factors.

c. Other faiths are true as far as they go, but they are incomplete, representing different levels of religious development. They need to be fulfilled by Christianity. Some who hold this view say that sincere believers in other religions may be Christians without carrying the name, and if they knew the fullness of Christian truth they would identify with it.

All through church history variations of these three views have been put forth. There has been no general agreement, and even today Christians disagree as to the right response to the question, "How do we interpret theologically the reality of other religions?" Fortunately, those Christians who are interested in creating interfaith community do not have to wait until agreement is reached on this question before they begin to build bridges of friendly communication between other believers and themselves. But let us look at the three general answers.

Those who hold to (a) are not much inclined to seek interfaith community. If one believes that other religions are plainly false, then the only course is to try to supplant them with the truth of Christianity. Many Christians hold this view. To them, believers in other faiths are people who need to be saved from error and converted to Christianity. While respecting their position, as well as the seriousness of their religious devotion, the way they interpret other religions puts an intolerable distance between themselves and those who believe differently. Even though they may profess a love for the other believers, their position is disastrous for human relations, since people of other faiths are viewed primarily as candidates for conversion, rather than as fellow human beings worthy of being listened to, possessing character, convictions, and hope. Their altogether negative assessment of other ways of believing usually means that they make little effort either to understand sympathetically the faith of others or to draw the others into open-hearted, unconditional friendship.

Option (b) seems promising and generous at first, but it surrenders too much. Taking all religions to be essentially the same brings them together in an unreal unity, blurring and trivializing the serious divergences that exist between them. Religion is not like a philosophy or ideology that people choose from a variety of possibilities. It is a part of the basic makeup of a group. Religion is so deeply ingrained in the history and way of life of its adherents that it can be called the key, or one of the keys, to a people's identity, and, by extension, to the identity of each individual believer. To maintain, as some do, that the various religions are alternate and equally valid paths to the same ultimate truth is to deny in some measure both the uniqueness of the identity of Christian faith and that of the members of the other religions. One might also say that if all religions are equally valid then they are self-contradictory, because in fact they are mutually exclusive in their beliefs and practices. This is the case even of the Baha'is and the Hindus, who believe in the unity of all religions. Their very belief in such unity sets them apart as exclusive and distinct. Also as evidence against the truth of option (b), we note that it is not possible for a believer to pass easily from one religion to another. Each faith tradition seems to demand complete loyalty.

Finally, we should question the theological basis for belief in the unity of all religions. The biblical witness strongly supports the exclusive and unique nature of Christian faith. Those who have staked their lives on the redemptive work of Jesus Christ and put their only hope in God's mercy as revealed in Christ cannot easily entertain thoughts of all religions being essentially the same.

The third answer, (c), seems less likely to be a hindrance to serious and fruitful exchanges between Christians and other believers. It has the virtue of appreciating other religions positively. However, to many it appears to be a domineering, triumphalistic attitude, since it seeks to bring all things under the heading of Christian. On the other hand, since this supposed reclaiming of all religions to the Christian side will take place at the end of time, belief in it need not hinder the progress of interfaith community in the present time. Biblically, this position seems to agree with the apostolic conviction that God will finally unify all things in Christ (see Ephesians 1:9,10). But it is not clear that other religions are a part of that future unifying of all things. The great summing up of ultimate truth may possibly take place even beyond and apart from religions.

All three of these general answers seem inadequate from the Christian point of view. As a fourth option I recommend that, in the interest of cultivating interfaith community, we leave the theological view of other religions as an open question. Many Christians confess they cannot explain how to interpret the existence of other faiths. So, let us be content to live with the uncertainty of our limited knowledge. It would be wise to join John Wesley in his cautious and biblical assessment of those men and women who live outside the Christian dispensation. In his sermon, "On Charity," he wrote more than 200 years ago:

> . . . we are not required to determine anything touching their final state. How it will please God, the Judge of all, to deal with them, we may leave to God himself. But this we know, that he is not the God of the Christians only, but the God of the Heathens also; that he is "rich in mercy to all that call upon him" according to the light they have; and that "in every nation he that feareth God and worketh righteousness is accepted of him."

And in the sermon, "On Living Without God," he wrote, "I have no authority from the Word of God 'to judge those that are without' . . . . It is far better to leave them to him that made them and who is 'the Father of the spirits of all flesh'." (Quotations from *The Sermons of John Wesley,* nos. 91 and 125, respectively)

Wesley's quotations from Scripture remind us of a number of fascinating hints in the Bible that God is at work in the world outside our Christian channels. For example, think of Cornelius in Acts 10, Melchizedek in Genesis 14, and Jesus' dealings with non-Jews. These are grounds for expectation and wonderment. We can hope all things (I Corinthians 13:7) and trust in the love and power of God in relation to all peoples of the earth. But we are not warranted to make conclusions about the members of any particular religious tradition. We can and must take seriously the expressions of faith that we hear from others. We can and must explore the depths of religious life outside Christianity. And yet, with all of that, we are always driven back to the unique fact that is the basis of our Christian identity: God has met us in Jesus Christ.

This position does not provide a well-defined place for other religions within the Christian view, but it has the advantage of making possible a free flow of mutually meaningful communication with those outside Christianity, simply because it does no violence either to the integrity of the Christian's faith identity or to that of the person from another religion.

FAITHFUL WITNESS

Continuing our exploration of resources in the Christian faith for creating interfaith community, we come to the question of interacting with others at a deep level of understanding. We Christians usually call this interaction by the name of witness, that is, bearing testimony to the love of God in Christ, but when seen in the light of encounter with other faith groups, Christian witness takes on a quality of depth that may be new to some. We all know that the act of witness consists of words, deeds, and attitudes. It is not simply projecting words toward other people, even if they are good words, without regard for the feelings of those who hear or receive the witness. And to know the background, way of life, and needs of people from other faiths is no light task. Yet, to be fair and friendly, true to our own principles of moral action, we must clothe our witness in interfaith understanding. In the process, we will no doubt be influenced by the witness (life, example, attitudes, words) of the others. This is especially true if we listen carefully to them.

This view of witness as a mutual exchange is exemplified in Christian holy Scriptures. The whole thrust of the Bible is that the almighty creator God entered into astonishingly close relations with human beings. Biblical history abounds in the record of acts and words streaming from the divine being and intended to stimulate a response in humankind. The divine witness calls forth a human witness. When people responded to this divine initiative, a personal, even intimate, dialogue came about between God and the human respondents. Whether in the stories of the patriarchs, or the prayers of the Psalms, or the dramatic struggles of the prophets, or the life of Jesus, or the meditations and letters of the apostles, this divine-human exchange or interaction is the very substance of the biblical record. When we realize that God in Christ is our model, when we meditate on the terms of this interaction, then we begin to understand the deep meaning of Christian witness, particularly in the case of interfaith community, that is, engaging in free and mutually meaningful exchanges with those of faiths other than ours. In interfaith communication, or mutual witness as we have described it, two parties do not necessarily have to agree with each other; but if they are sincerely looking for interfaith community, they will at least expect their understanding of each other to deepen so that whatever they do together, in community, will have greater weight.

FACING THE DEMANDS OF TRUTH

Inevitably, as believers in different religions get together and witness to what is most precious in their traditions, there will be a confrontation between "truths"—my truth versus your truth. As full of good will as we might be, we cannot avoid the following questions: "In the interest of interreligious peace and understanding are we compromising the truth? Is truth, after all, merely relative? Or is there an absolute truth not made by humankind?"

We Christians usually say, yes, there is certainly an absolute truth whose source is the God of truth. But our tradition puts us on guard against presumptuous handling of what we might suppose to be the absolute truth. The Apostle Paul wrote that in his missionary activity he was not a peddler of God's Word, but that he spoke "in Christ," that is, in an environment of truth (II Corinthians 2:17). He was not, then, a propagandist pushing "truths" for which he made absolute claims, but rather a person who spoke humbly out of his exposure to the light of truth. The deeper that we delve into the truth to which we have been exposed, the more we are aware that it is not something that we can know, that is, enclose within the framework of our mind. Truth is more of a setting or environment in which we have put ourselves by the decision of our minds and wills. We do not possess the truth, but it possesses us to the degree that is passed on to us by Jesus Christ. We are completely dependent on God's act in sending Christ for our grasp of truth. It is no wonder that we find him incomparable. No matter how tolerant we may be of other ways of believing, we are still consumed by the incomparability of Christ. We can scarcely be Christian and think otherwise.

How then, taken up as we are with the matchless Christ, can we avoid coming into conflict with those of other faiths, who hold to what they consider to be matchless expressions of truth, the Koran for Muslims, or the wisdom of the Buddha, or the Hindu Scriptures? Are we not, by our exclusive insistence on the uniqueness of Christ, making practically impossible any kind of effective interfaith community? To answer this question, let us remember that the truth is greater than all of us. Then as we humbly and loyally rally around the person who is our point of contact, that is, Jesus Christ, we should expect others to affirm those points of contact with the truth that make them what they are: Jews, Muslims, Sikhs, Hindus, or whatever. For interfaith community to succeed, we must all confess that these distinctive points are places of contact only, not the absolute truth itself. Then we will be in a position to let the truth speak and exert its attractive power. The important thing is that we should learn to do this together, without surrendering in any sense the uniqueness of our religions, but affirming together that the truth to which we open ourselves is greater than our grasp of it.

DEALING WITH DIFFERENCES

As we become partners in the quest for interfaith community and develop a dialogue with others, we will perceive certain differences, whether in belief or in practice, that separate us. Christians need to draw upon the resources of their faith to deal with this sense of difference. We are not saying how other believers should react to differences. That is their affair.

Differences may be described generally as either doctrinal or practical. Doctrinal matters have to do with the mind, with beliefs. If we Christians explain carefully what we believe, those from other faiths ought to understand what we say about our doctrines, even if some of the things we hold to are shrouded in the divine mystery. And similarly, if we Christians listen carefully to adherents of other faiths, we will understand what they believe. This sounds simple, but it is precisely that careful listening to one another that has usually not taken place. If we listen to each other, we will take a great step toward a friendly, constructive relationship. But this is only a first step. An important part of the doctrinal difficulty between people of faith is the fact that we not only want others to understand us, but we also want them to believe as we do. This is only natural, since we consider our religious faith as a precious gift to be shared with all. However, if we exert pressure to get others to believe as we do or impose our beliefs on them, we make it hard, if not impossible, to create interfaith community. We must give up the insistence that others become like ourselves. Notice that this does not mean giving up a vital witness to one's faith. It only means leaving the other free to be himself or herself.

Besides doctrinal differences, there are practical problems between members of different faiths. In the practices of different religions, certain elements seem unacceptable to us North American Christians. Usually these are things having to do with cultures about which we know little. Customs and values in other countries—family traditions, relations between the sexes, hospitality and etiquette, attitudes toward authority, the feeling of community, and habits of eating and drinking and dress—are often strange to us, and they affect the way people practice their religion. Many have been in the U.S. for only a few years and have not changed their customs. So often what appears to be a practical difference between religions is only a cultural one, and upon investigation we find it to be no obstacle to interfaith community. And, by the same token, if we listen carefully to others, we may find that some of our cultural practices present problems to our would-be partners in community.

In the final analysis there may be some practical differences that cannot be resolved by patient efforts at understanding. However, even the irreducible problems of difference can be dealt with in Christian faith. We must call upon the power of Christian love to enable us to bear the burden of divergence that cannot be overcome. A part of the genius of Christian faith is the ability to get under the burden of great difficulties and by patient, thoughtful endurance and dialogue to nullify the effect of their alienating power. This does not mean that one side or the other has to give in. It means that they live together in a friendly and harmonious relationship that satisfies the demands both of love and of truth, especially truth lived as much as asserted.

ALL THINGS MERGE

Millions of sparks arise from a fire and, after existing separately, finally merge in it. Innumerable dust particles arise from the dust and will again become dust. Millions of waves arise on a large body of water, but the waves on water still remain water. The same way, from the infinite state, forms arise out of the formless and arising from it will all merge in it.

—Adi Granth

Sikhism

caption for faced page: The Rehnberg Memorial Window of The Unitarian Universalist Church, Rockford, Illinois; designed by Frank Houtkamp, 1974.

4

Some Active Interfaith Communities

The history of interfaith community does not begin with us. Even though it is a relatively new concept in our country, a surprisingly large number of interfaith community efforts exist. In this chapter I shall describe some of these as models so that readers may have a better idea of what is being done by people of different faiths talking and working together, and also how they are carrying out their projects. The models that I describe show that interfaith community has acquired status as an institution in some cases, whereas in others the efforts remain tentative, in the exploratory state. Many may not become permanent, organized communities. Short-lived, partial, incomplete, even unsuccessful, attempts to create interfaith community can be important in the overall picture.

If there is one phrase to characterize all efforts it is "personal contact." We must be in contact with each other before there can be any hope of community. And yet that is the very thing that was lacking in the past. We talked about other religions and their adherents. We judged and assessed them. We even studied them. We compared them with ourselves. But we did it in their absence. Likewise, of course, they did the same in our absence. In the present-day multireligious U.S., we have an opportunity at last to meet one another.

In the last chapter I shall give some detailed suggestions on how to make contact. But the models we describe in this chapter are animated by people of various faiths who are already happily in touch with each other. Some would say that a better word to characterize our efforts would be "dialogue." But I reserve that treasured word to describe a level of interfaith community that is only reached after much effort. Dialogue, in the sense of mutually meaningful discourse, is fairly rare. Much of the time we are talking to others, not with them. But I am sure that from time to time personal contact does deepen into dialogue, especially when some interfaith task so absorbs our minds and energies that we are humble enough to listen as well as to speak to others. More will be said about dialogue in the next chapter.

Two friends can constitute a simple interfaith community, informal as it is. A rabbi and a priest, teacher and child, two teachers, schoolmates, neighbors, partners at sports, club members, technicians, and professionals. The unselfconscious interaction of two friends may not seem to accomplish much in the way of social purpose, but to explore one another's faith experience in this way may be the finest kind of interfaith community.

From one-to-one encounters to organized occasions for discussion and hoped-for dialogue is a big step. Sometimes a tragic event or other momentous happening serves as the impetus for getting together as a group. After the 2001 terrorist attacks in the U.S., some Muslim, Jewish, and Christian women began to meet regularly in Greensboro, North Carolina. Their immediate purpose was to seek mutual understanding after the shocking events of September 11. The Reverend Mark Sills, a United Methodist pastor in Greensboro, reported that the meetings of these women are sponsored by Faith/Action, a local interfaith organization, and that the women's conversations have moved toward sharing in cooking techniques across ethnic lines. Sills hopes that eventually women from other faiths will join the group. (United Methodist News Service, February 4, 2002)

By contrast, members of the Muslim Council of New England have for 12 years engaged Christians of the Massachusetts Council of Churches in dialogue sessions, held three times a year. About 25 or so regular participants, with occasional visitors, discuss a topic of common interest chosen in advance. Two brief introductions to the topic are given, one by a Muslim and one by a Christian. Then free-moving exchanges follow, guided by a chairperson. The Reverend Betsy Sowers of Westboro, Massachusetts, coordinator from the Christian side, noted that the discussants usually choose subjects of practical and social concern, rather than strictly theological questions. The group has dealt with human rights; the place of women in society; abortion; physician-assisted suicide; social justice; and Abraham, Moses, and Jesus. Dr. Karim Khudairi of Wellesley, Massachusetts, the Muslim coordinator, said that through the years a good deal of mutual trust has developed as the same participants have come to know and appreciate each other.

Ms. Betty Gamble of the United Methodist General Commission on Christian Unity and Interreligious Concerns conveyed a report from faraway Jerusalem, scene of so much strife and violence. It told of a Women's Interfaith Encounter, bringing Jewish, Christian, and Muslim women together for their second monthly meeting in February 2002. They discussed a topic of spiritual and social concern, "The creation of women in the Bible and the Koran and how it affects the way religions relate to women." Those present were students, professionals, and homemakers, ranging in age from 25 to 70 years old. One person from each of the three religions gave an initial presentation from her background, and then the participants divided into small groups for lively discussion, with a warm spirit of good will and humor prevailing. Quoting from the report:

The Jewish presenter stated that she had gone through the religious school system and studied the story of creation any times, but had never been given the sources that she found to present to us. A Muslim woman said that her study of the Koran in preparation for the meeting not only strengthened her appreciation of her religion but strengthened her feminism. A Catholic nun was surprised to learn new interpretations of the creation of woman that she had never heard before.

Subsequent gatherings of this women's group have dealt with such subjects as "Education for Women in the Three Faiths" and "The Founding Mothers of the Religions." The Women's Interfaith Encounter is a project of a larger interfaith community in the Middle East called Interfaith Encounter Association, founded in 2001. (For information about its history and its other projects, see "Contacts" at the end of this chapter.)

In several cities of California, Jewish and Arab Americans (including of course, both Muslims and Christians) meet regularly for what are called "living room dialogues," in order to get to know each other better and to discuss the anguishing political situation in the Middle East. As they eat together and share details of their daily life, their hopes and fears, all in the light of their religious differences and similarities, they are doing their part to prepare for peace between Israel and her neighbors. (*Christian Science Monitor*, February 6, 2002)

The United States Conference of Roman Catholic Bishops maintains a secretariat for Ecumenical and Interreligious Affairs located in Washington, D.C. From that center, Catholics encourage and support numerous interreligious dialogues of an ongoing nature throughout the country. Regional organizations in the various dioceses bring people from different religions together for discussions on a variety of subjects. For example, every year three regional Muslim-Catholic meetings take place in the Midwest, on the West Coast, and in the Midatlantic.

Of particular note has been a series of Buddhist-Catholic conferences, sponsored and inspired by the Benedictine-Trappist Monastic Interreligious Dialogue (see "Contacts" at the end of this chapter). The prominent monastic tradition in both faiths, stressing seclusion, asceticism, and celibacy, naturally contributed to the desire of both Buddhist and Catholic monastics to get to know each other better. From the Catholic side the well-known Trappist monk, Thomas Merton, an author and poet who died in 1968, proved a strong influence to encourage interaction between the two faiths. Merton once observed, "I do not believe that I could understand our Christian faith the way I understand it if it were not for the light of Buddhism." (Mitchell and Wiseman, eds., *The Gethsemani Encounter,* cited in chapter 2)

And from the Buddhist side the Dalai Lama, world leader of the Tibetan Buddhists, has for years encouraged his coreligionists to seek interaction with Christians. After several years of preparation, 25 Catholics and 25 Buddhists, almost all of the monastic tradition, met in 1996 at the Gethsemani Monastery in Kentucky, where Thomas Merton lived. For five days the participants heard speakers from both religions dealing with many aspects of the spiritual life, and engaged in intense discussion and acts of worship according to the two faith traditions. They found that the monastic ideal in the two religions is the same, but that Buddhists and Catholics live out that ideal in quite different ways having to do with such things as group organization, priorities in daily life, and avenues of service. The papers presented at Gethsemani proved to be of such a high caliber that they were published for the benefit of the wider public as *The Gethsemani Encounter*.

Since 1996 other such gatherings on a smaller scale have taken place in various localities, and in 2002 a second Gethsemani Encounter was held. These Buddhists and Christians in dialogue reached a deep level of mutual sympathy and understanding, in large part because of the way they performed their acts of worship in such close community, and with such profound respect for each other's particular form of prayer. This was accomplished without any compromise of either Christian or Buddhist distinctiveness. The Gethsemani examples are special in that they involve mostly clergy from the two religions and are based on a particular common interest, that is, the monastic way of life. The Catholic monastics are planning together how to make the results of the encounters accessible to the rest of the church. Such occurrences illustrate how groups of limited or broad common concern can with profit organize an interfaith exchange of views. More specific advice on this course of action with follow in chapter 5.

An unusual type of interfaith community is two jazz musicians in Connecticut who are making music together and in dialogue as men of faith. David Chevan, bassist and professor of music at Southern Connecticut State University, New Haven, is Jewish. His partner, Warren Byrd, jazz pianist, is a professor in the Connecticut area and a Christian from the African American culture. They have recorded sacred music from their respective traditions, and the results have been widely acclaimed. As they blend spirituals and Jewish folk religious songs, they seek to show the kinship of joy, passion, and suffering in the two cultural strands. The two musicians insist that their collaboration is no gimmick, but that it is an interfaith effort. Both artists are passionate about their religion. Chevan describes some of the dynamics of their musical and verbal conversations, as quoted by critic, George Robinson: "Dialogues don't stand still. There have been nights when we just won't see eye to eye. Dialogue is like that. We are deliberately bringing in this other agenda going on with the music. It's not always going to be agreement. On the other hand, when you get two people who respect and value each other, it's going to be at a pretty interesting level." (For more on Robinson, see "Contacts" at the end of this chapter.)

Interfaith prayer is a more formalized setting for interfaith community than simply talking together. Many of us are familiar with the common interfaith prayer service held at Thanksgiving. This is a favorable moment, since Thanksgiving is religiously neutral, not specific to any particular faith, and yet it emphasizes the value of gratitude, something common to all religious systems.

Nestled among the towering skyscrapers of downtown Dallas, Texas, is a unique place called Thanks-Giving Square, the home of the Center for World Thanksgiving. Amid the tranquil beauty of courtyard, gardens, and fountains stands a chapel with a distinctive spiral tower. Since 1981, the year of its establishment, the center has, through its programs, held up the value of gratitude expressed in thanksgiving, calling attention to its central importance in all religions and cultures of the world. Thanks-Giving Square is a place where people from many backgrounds can "use thanksgiving as a way to heal division and enhance mutual understanding." Ms. Ebby Halliday Acers, speaking at Thanks-Giving Square in 2001, quoted the late Albert Outler, the eminent United Methodist scholar, as saying, "[G]iving thanks is the purest moral energy we humans have." And because it is universal, the giving of thanks constitutes perhaps the best theme for testing the possibilities of praying together as believers whose manners of worship in general are starkly diverse and even incompatible. (For the source of quotes and other information, see "Contacts" at the end of this chapter.)

Originally, back in 1961, the Dallas City Planning Council conceived the idea of setting aside a parcel of land to celebrate some important human value or quality of life. Gratitude, or thanksgiving, was chosen as the theme, and through the years religious leaders, educators, and philosophers from many nations were invited to concentrate their efforts in Dallas on highlighting the ways in which people express gratitude. A board of private citizens manages the center, and its efforts are supported by contributions from the public. An advisory board representing 30 different religions and denominations helps the full-time staff in developing programs, organizing study conferences, and holding regular celebrations of thanksgiving. In Dallas, the center operates an interfaith program with members from more then ten world religions to discuss religious diversity and other issues. Through its Multifaith Exploration and Exchange Program, local people meet twice a month for five months each year to practice interaction between religious groups by visitation, study, and dialogue. The chapel at Thanks-Giving Square is used regularly by religious groups in the Dallas area. In 2002, an Episcopal eucharistic celebration and a Muslim communal prayer service were held each week. Periodically the center hosts an international Convocation of World Thanksgiving, welcoming religious leaders and scholars from many countries. Educational materials dealing with the nature of gratitude and the social values of good interfaith relations are provided by the staff for children and youth. The Center for World Thanksgiving is an interfaith community, based on praying together, that has become a sustained, institutionalized part of life in Dallas, and whose influence extends to other parts of the world.

Other than expressing gratitude together at Thanksgiving, any time of crisis in the nation or in the community can be a call to communal prayer by religious people of all persuasions. The tragic events of September 11, 2001, have resulted in innumerable prayer services throughout the country. Often these have taken the form of prayer breakfasts, like one held in Hartford, Connecticut. Attended by five hundred people, the service was a time not only for specific prayers, but also for hearing speakers from the Islamic, Sikh, Hindu, Buddhist, Jewish, and Christian religions speak about how each of them stands for tolerance and justice. (*Hartford Courant,* November 8, 2001)

And in Houston, Texas, at an interfaith prayer service, Sayeed Siddiqui, president of the Islamic Society of Greater Houston, said:

Thousands of fellow Americans have lost their lives. Many more are injured and horrified at the disaster at the World Trade Center. There are physical injuries, and then there are spiritual injuries. Physical injuries will eventually heal, but spiritual injuries have left a scar for life. The only way to ease some of this pain is for all of us to come in the comforting shadow of Almighty God, asking for his grace, asking for justice, and then, to be forgiving and patient. Our real test is the patience and restraint we have to exercise no matter how angry we are. We are hurt, but we have to forgive. We condemn the horrific act of terrorism. We unite with the families who have been victimized. Sanctity of life is very important in Islam. All of us are created by Almighty God to worship him, and the way to worship him in Islam is to serve humanity in the best possible manner with love and compassion. We stand with you fellow Americans hand in hand to support each other through this difficult period of healing. We are Americans just like you and pray to the same Creator and are hurting just like you. Let us join our hands in prayer and support our government in seeking justice. (*Houston Chronicle,* September 14, 2001)

Missing of course on such occasions, were special postures, formulas, and images, the elements that make up communal prayer in any one faith tradition. This observation points out a difficulty with interfaith prayer, a subject that will receive more attention in the next chapter. Whatever the awkwardness that we may feel about joining other religious groups for prayer, this model remains basic to our efforts to create interfaith community. A common impulse to pray together moves us all from time to time.

SERVING TOGETHER

All religions stress the importance of service to others as a basic duty, so it is no wonder that many models of interfaith community exist in which people of different faiths unite, because of their spiritual convictions, to serve other people. The types of service rendered are as varied as are human needs.

Mall of America in Bloomington, Minnesota, is the largest shopping mall in the United States. For more than ten years, an interfaith community called Mall Area Religious Council (MARC) has provided a spiritual presence in that great marketplace. Twenty-eight congregations have joined MARC, including Catholic, Protestant, Muslim, Baha'i, Buddhist, Christian Science, Eckankar,

Unitarian Universalist, and Unity. Hindus and Jews take part on a consultation basis. This interfaith community came into being after careful negotiation with mall authorities. On the one hand, the mall recognizes its own interest in having a link with the community through an interfaith coalition. On the other hand, MARC is in no sense an official arm of mall management. For example, it does not provide a chaplaincy for the mall. Sometimes the people living around the mall feel threatened by its massive presence, and MARC helps to provide an avenue of communication between the mall and the residents. Also the authorities welcome the interfaith group's help in preventing the possible use of the mall premises by some religious groups to engage in proselytizing among the crowds.

MARC's vision and programs are relatively modest in that it seeks to provide in this somewhat unusual setting "a broad-based spiritual presence…embodying the values of understanding, community, dignity, respect, and peace." Through interfaith cooperation, it furnishes information about the different religions and their presence in the community. To that end, a sign reading "Where to Worship" is displayed prominently in the mall announcing the places of gathering of member congregations. Pockets on the sign contain customized placards for each place listed so that visitors may help themselves to pertinent information. Once a year in the late autumn, a three-day exhibit called Holy Day Holidays is shown to mall visitors, giving facts about and insight into the celebrations of different world religions. A permanent information center dealing with religious diversity is under development.

Early in 2002 the Mall of America management consulted with MARC to provide a meditation room for mall employees. This place of quietness is open to all religious faiths. MARC provided a large Golden Rule Poster to hang on one wall, giving quotations from the Scriptures of thirteen religions that convey the message of the Golden Rule. On another wall of the meditation room hangs a compass providing orientation for those faiths, such as Islam, that prescribe prayer to be performed facing in a particular direction. In addition there is a space for performing ritual ablutions adjacent to the meditation room.

The Mall Area Religious Council is governed by a council of representatives of member groups. All those engaged in the council's work are unpaid volunteers. This cooperative witness has established a solid place in the mall, and it distinguishes itself as an original model of interfaith community making its witness and rendering its service in the heart of a mighty "temple" of consumerism.

A heart-warning story lies behind another service model, this one in Ramle, Israel. In the 1930s a Palestinian Muslim, Ahmed al-Khayri, built a home for his family in Ramle, situated between Tel Aviv and Jerusalem. Then when the state of Israel was founded in 1948, war came. Mr. al-Khayri and family were expelled from Ramle, and the home was confiscated by the Israelis. A family named Ashkenazi, Jewish immigrants from Bulgaria, was given the property, which they later purchased from the government. Then, years later, after the war of 1967, Mr. al-Khayri and family returned to see their old home. There they met Dalia Ashkenazi, a university student and the only person at home at the time. Dalia heard the story of how the al-Khayris had been forcibly put out of the house that later became her home. There developed a friendship between the two families over the years. Dalia finally inherited the home and married an American Jewish immigrant, Yehezkil Landau. Then the al-Khayris and the Landaus decided to dedicate the house to social service for the children of Ramle and eventually for adults as well. They named the center "Open House," engaged the services of an educator, and organized tutoring programs for school children; summer camps for Arabs and Jews; and training in crafts, language classes, and discussion groups. In recent years Open House has received international recognition and support. It stands as a witness to interfaith peace and understanding in a region torn by strife. One of the directors wrote, "Jews and Palestinians are called to sanctify the land together by ending the bloodshed, the injustice, the suffering of both peoples. That can only happen when people's hearts are transformed, when fear is supplanted by trust, anger by forgiveness, and grief by compassion for the suffering of others." (*Holy Land Magazine,* spring 1995; see "Contacts" at the end of this chapter for more information on Friends of Open House.)

Wichita, Kansas, is the site of an interfaith community called Inter-Faith Ministries, whose primary focus is on social services. Inter-Faith Ministries is an outgrowth of the former Wichita Ministerial Alliance, which after welcoming Jewish, Roman Catholic, and Orthodox membership, gradually enlarged its scope until, in 1978, it changed its name to Wichita Inter-Faith Ministries. Today it includes as members congregations of eight world religions: Baha'ism, Buddhism, Christianity, Hinduism, Islam, Judaism, Native American, and Universal Unitarianism. Supported financially by member groups, grants from foundations, and donations from the public, Inter-Faith Ministries devotes itself single-mindedly to a range of programs addressing many of the major needs of society. Here are some of its current projects:

1. Addresses racism by training congregations and organizations to discern race prejudice in their midst and to eliminate it.

2. Works on a campaign to end childhood hunger by raising public awareness, supporting food security systems, and seeking to eliminate the basic causes of hunger, including poverty.

3. Maintains personnel trained to intervene quickly if the Wichita area should be visited by sudden disaster.

4. Runs two shelters for local homeless persons.

5. Has provided, in its newly constructed Inter-Faith Villa, 37 units of permanent low-cost housing, along with supportive services, for persons in need.

6. Sponsors a local chapter of Mother to Mother, bringing together women from different national and cultural backgrounds to strengthen community ties.

7. Receives first-time juvenile offenders referred by the district attorney's office, arranges meetings between offenders and the victims with a view to reconciliation, counsels offenders and their families, and helps arrange programs of restitution involving community service by the offenders.

For these and other programs, Inter-Faith Ministries requires a staff and regular volunteers numbering about 30. For special campaigns and projects, dozens of volunteers come from the Wichita area to help. (For more information, see "Contacts" at the end of this chapter.)

Another way in which interfaith efforts center on serving together is in the sharing of buildings or meeting spaces. Several examples of Christian-Jewish and Christian-Muslim cooperation along this line can be found. Usually it is a matter of the majority faith, Christianity, agreeing with the minority one for sharing the facilities of a church property, either for a limited period of time or permanently. This kind of mutual service to the communities involved reached a new level, however, when, according to a press report, Jews and Presbyterians in Maryland agreed to share jointly the $3 million financial burden for renovating the aging Bradley Hills Presbyterian Church. This practical cooperation is the culmination of a relationship between the Presbyterians and Bethesda Jewish Congregation of many years duration. In the renovated building there is a room specially designed for Jewish worship, but which can also be used by the Christians for informal gatherings and classes. The main sanctuary for Christian worship can also serve Jews on High Holidays and both congregations jointly at Thanksgiving. The pastor of Bradley Hills Church, the Reverend Susan Andrews, said that in spite of the close relationship between the two congregations, they are clearly quite different families of faith. They make no attempt to blend their separate theologies but simply share their values for the good of the larger community. (*Hartford Courant,* May 11, 2002)

In a world so weary of violence and war, it is only natural that peace and justice should be a rallying point for people of faith in their efforts to serve humanity together. One of the oldest such efforts is the Fellowship of Reconciliation, started in 1915 as a Christian organization, but developing through the years into an international movement in more than 40 countries and showing an interreligious membership of Jews, Buddhists, Christians, and Muslims. In the name of their respective faiths, the people of the Fellowship of Reconciliation stand straightforwardly for nonviolence. They are testing "the power of love and truth for resolving human conflict," to quote from their website, www.forusa.org. In the pursuit of their aims, they have confronted head-on such intractable problems as Iraq, Palestine, Colombia, and Vieques, Puerto Rico. They have shown solidarity with victims of injustice, worked for more humane criminal justice systems, advocated practices of ecological conservation, and opposed participation in warfare.

We may gain some idea of how concerned people are about peace and justice through the communications network Interfaith Voices for Peace and Justice. Its website lists 741 faith-based organizations that direct their energies toward issues of peace and justice. However, Interfaith Voices gives "interfaith" a different meaning from the one we give to it. We limit the sense of "interfaith" to "between or among faiths." Many of the 741 organizations listed are clearly confessional, that is, belonging to one particular religious perspective. So, to bring that list into line with our use of "interfaith," it would be more appropriate to call it a "multifaith" list with names of religious groups, interfaith or not, that are working for peace and justice. Strictly speaking, "multifaith" means simply "many faiths," regardless of whether they are in communication with one another or not, whereas "interfaith" refers to inter-action or a relationship between two or more faiths. (For the web address, see "Contacts" at the end of this chapter.)

Serving together in the broadest sense are a number of large, well-established coalitions that concentrate on bringing many social services to the greatest number possible of those people who are their focus. For example, Interfaith Ministries for Greater Houston, Texas, represents Baha'i, Buddhist, Christian, Hindu, Jewish, Muslim, Sikh, Unitarian Universalist, and Zoroastrian believers who provide services for children, sen-iors, and refugees. They have 30 years' experi-ence, 160 employees, and 3,000 volunteers who minister to 500,000 people a year. Their support comes from both the public and the private sector.

A quick review of some details of their work will provide excellent examples of what is possi-ble when an interfaith community decides to ren-der social service.

For children, Houston's members of Interfaith Ministries help victims of abuse, provide mentors and tutors for children in and out of their schools, and send volunteer foster grandparents to help those in special need. For seniors, they deliver meals and give support services to the home-bound, provide groceries once a week to those with low incomes, and give instruction in how to use Medicare advantageously and how to take medications. For refugees, they train volunteers to sponsor and support those who have recently arrived in the U.S.; help them to find housing and employment and to obtain English-language instruction; and otherwise guide the new arrivals in adjusting to the culture. To nurture the spiritual exchanges between participants in the service pro-grams, Interfaith Ministries provides structured opportunities for the different faith communities to visit each other and learn through observation and conversation the ways in which the particular religions carry on their communal life. (See "Contacts" at the end of this chapter for the web address.)

Some interfaith communities take several differ-ent forms, depending on their organization and stated goals. A great many began as Christian clergy associations or local ecumenical councils of churches. Then after a time they welcomed the Jewish communities into their midst, often with-out changing their name. In recent years some such organizations have broadened their member-ship to include still other faiths, and they have log-ically changed their name to interfaith councils or interfaith associations. Of course this change has involved a widening of their activities as they seek dialogue, practice praying together, and serve community needs together.

A different pattern of development evolved in Hartford, Connecticut, which has resulted in an interfaith community called the Connecticut Committee for Interreligious Understanding (CCIU). Membership on the committee includes Baha'is, Buddhists, Christians, Hindus, Muslims, Jews, Sikhs, and Unitarian Universalists. Independent of any previously existing councils of churches or clergy associations, this effort began when a group of individuals met in 1994 to plan for a program, including a service of worship, to celebrate the 50th anniversary of the United Nations. Encouraged by that event, they have held other conferences and developed programs to help Hartford residents get acquainted with the religious diversity of the area.

As the Reverend Richard Griffis of West Hartford wrote in 1997, "We live in a time when many more of us than ever before want to understand more than just the sacred traditions in which we are at home. We grow wiser in our own faith commitments by having been drawn toward others in their faith communities." In their desire to be of service to the larger community, members of the group have taken a public stand on issues of interreligious concern. On January 22, 2002, they cooperated with Archbishop David A. Cronin of the Roman Catholic Church to sponsor an interreligious prayer service for world peace.

Nimal Singh of the Connecticut Sikh Association wrote, "The Connecticut Committee for Interreligious Understanding is a young group with very limited resources. I enjoy participating in our conversations and other events and celebrations. I learn from the perspectives of other faith traditions—as we confront problems and issues—and sometimes I gain a deeper understanding of certain dimensions of my own faith. I hope that we can reach more and more people. May they find that, in spite of our diverse images, as Bhakt Kabir (in the Sikh holy Scripture) said, 'All of us have emanated from the same eternal flame.'" (CCIU newsletter, April 2001; for more information see "Contacts" at the end of this chapter.)

Laguna Niguel, California, is home to an unusual interfaith community called Alliance for Spiritual Community. It began in 1991 and has on its board of directors members of the following religious groups: Baha'i, Buddhist, Christian, Islam, Judaism, Native American, New Thought, and Vedanta. It is supported by donations from participants in its programs and the interested public.

Although the alliance is an interfaith community itself, according to the meaning defined in this book, it exists solely for the purpose of strengthening community in any place or situation within its reach. It does this by emphasizing the spiritual nature of community. Its activities include educational events, especially those relating to the different cultures in our country; celebrations such as Global Peacemaking; and, especially, organized interfaith dialogue meetings. Under the leadership of its president and founding director, Kay Lindahl, the alliance has done outstanding work in helping people seeking to deepen their community experience through dialogue. In the next chapter we shall consider some of the suggestions for dialogue produced by the Alliance for Spiritual Community. (For more information see "Contacts" at the end of this chapter.)

Like the Connecticut Committee for Interreligious Understanding, another group arose as the result of a worldwide celebration. In Columbia, South Carolina, the Department of Religious Studies of the University of South Carolina invited representatives of several religious communities in the state to help plan an interfaith conference to coincide with the 1993 centennial celebration of the World's Parliament of Religions held in Chicago. Baha'is, Buddhists, Christians, Hindus, Jews, Muslims, and Unitarian Universalists took part in that conference. They were so energized that they decided to continue as an organized interfaith initiative. Eventually South Carolina Sikhs and Native Americans joined them. Named Partners in Dialogue, this interfaith community has its office at the University of South Carolina, and its director is Carl Evans, professor in the Department of Religious Studies.

Partners in Dialogue has continued to hold annual conferences on various topics of interfaith concern, with the chair of each gathering held by a representative of one of the member faiths. As its name indicates, this interfaith community focuses on dialogue, primarily using potluck suppers as the occasion for drawing people together. Different ethnic foods are served, and in this informal atmosphere a panel discussion or other presentation introduces the subject for discussion.

Besides the conference and dialogue settings for its efforts, Partners in Dialogue also is involved in social service projects of an interesting nature. When South Carolina was torn by controversy a few years ago over the flying of the Confederate flag atop the state capitol, Partners in Dialogue launched a "Witness for Reconciliation," trying from the interfaith perspective to heal the racial divisions in the state. With the state Department of Corrections, it joined other groups to give interfaith support for families of prison inmates who are terminally ill. It has joined a coalition of religious groups to articulate the meaning of religious freedom in the pluralistic culture of South Carolina.

(For more information, see "Contacts" at the end of this chapter.)

In our nation's capital, we find another interfaith community manifesting several forms. For 20 years the Interfaith Conference of Metropolitan Washington has carried on its work through a coalition of faith groups. The member groups and public donations support the Interfaith Conference. The Vision Statement of this organization states: "We come together because our love for God and humanity inspires it; our concern for justice, freedom, and peace demands it; and what we can learn from each other requires it. Baha'i, Hindu, Islamic, Jewish, Latter-Day Saints, Protestant, Roman Catholic, and Sikh, through our collaboration in the Interfaith Conference [we] intend to be a symbol of moral unity in a broken world." A listing of some of the projects and activities of this dynamic community helps to broaden and deepen our grasp of what is possible through interfaith community. The conference:

- Holds an annual public dialogue especially for the laity.
- Conducts interfaith prayer services every year on the birthday of Martin Luther King, Jr., as well as on special occasions of need or crisis.
- Prepares religious education materials on interfaith subjects.
- Organizes visits to various places of worship.
- Provides a forum where people of faith can speak out with one voice on moral concerns.
- Sponsors an annual interfaith concert of sacred music from the various religious traditions.
- Prepares annually a directory of emergency food and shelter sources in Washington, with United Way printing 10,000 copies.
- Builds coalitions to aid the poor and homeless, women and children.

• Works with other groups to overcome racial and ethnic tensions.

Readers will have been struck by the variety of ways in which interfaith community occurs. I hope that the examples in this chapter will give those who want to create interfaith community ideas that they can apply to their own situation. These ideas, taken with the suggestions to be offered in the last chapter, should enable readers to plan concrete steps that they can take to begin the experience of getting to know believers in another faith.

CONTACTS

• Alliance for Spiritual Community, **www.asc-spiritualcommunity.org**

• Benedictine-Trappist Monastic Interreligious Dialogue, **http://www.monasticdialog.com**

• Center for World Thanksgiving, **http://www.thanksgiving.org**

• Connecticut Committee for Interreligious Understanding, 77 Sherman Street, Hartford, CT 06105

• Friends of Open House, P.O. Box 1014, Great Barrington, MA 01230

• George Robinson, **www.georgerobinson.freeservers.com/Music.html**

• Interfaith Conference of Washington [D.C.], **www.interfaith-metrodc.org**

• Interfaith Encounter Association, **http://www.interfaith-encounter.org**

• Interfaith Ministries for Greater Houston, **www.imgh.org**

• Inter-Faith Ministries, Wichita, Kansas, **http://www.ifmnet.org**; (316) 264-9303

• Interfaith Voices, **www.interfaithvoices.org**

• Mall Area Religious Council, **http://www.meaningstore.org**

• The Golden Rule poster is for sale by Conexus Multifaith Media, **http://www.conexuspress.com**; (877) 784-7779

• Partners in Dialogue, **www.cla.sc.edu** "Partners in Dialogue" in the search box for USC.

LOVING KINDNESS

As a mother at the risk of her life watches over her own child, her only child, so let every one cultivate a boundless (friendly) mind toward all beings. And let him cultivate good will towards all the world, a boundless (friendly) mind, above and below and across, unobstructed, without hatred, without enmity.

—Sutra Nipata

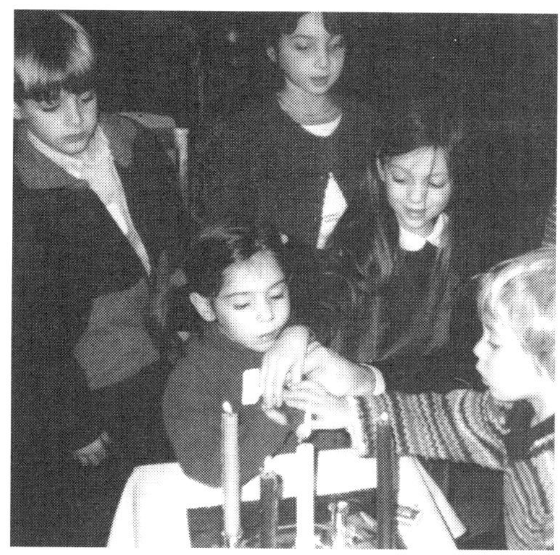

5

PRACTICAL SUGGESTIONS

After having learned about the range of interfaith communities that exist across our nation, many readers may want to join such efforts where it is possible. They will ask, "How can we start such a community?" or "How do we take the preliminary steps toward creating interfaith community?" You will remember that in the last chapter we noted that the common feature of all such interfaith efforts is personal contact. And this is what any concerned Christian can begin with. The step to take toward joining other people of faith in conversation or service together is simply to reach out in friendship to one or several members of religions other than our own.

Some may feel, however, that the descriptive sketches of the other faiths given in chapter 1 of this book are hardly sufficient to equip them for going deeper into the matter. They may feel the need to know more about those other faiths and more about the Christian spiritual and theological background for interfaith relations. Here are some opportunities for learning:

1. The internet is a veritable gold mine for gaining information and insight. Type the name of a religion in your search engine's window and you will find many interesting sites to visit. The information is usually presented in an easy-to-understand way, often illustrated with scenes depicting the worship life and practices of the religion in question, as well as examples of its graphic and literary art.

2. Everybody knows about the public library as a place of learning, and the reference librarian can point you to sources for audiovisual mate-

rials on the world religions.

3. Do not forget museums of art and ethnology. Many people know about the great collections like the Metropolitan Museum of Art in New York City, but smaller museums exist as well that display excellent exhibits relating to the religions of humankind. Two examples are the Richmond, Virginia, Museum of Fine Arts and the Milwaukee, Wisconsin, Ethnological Museum.

4. Take advantage of lectures, symposia, and conferences having to do with one religion or with the multireligious nature of our society.

5. The National Council of the Churches of Christ in the U.S.A. has made available two publications of great value for our subject. An 11-page policy statement is entitled, "Interfaith Relations and the Churches," and for study groups a guide to reflection and action is called, "Interfaith Relations and Christian Living." (See "Resources" at the end of this chapter for information on ordering these materials.)

One can hope, though, that sooner or later readers, moved by the theme of this book, will pass from study to the actual process of creating interfaith community. For the following suggestions, let us maintain the same progression of thought that we followed in chapter 4, that is, talking together, first of all, then praying together, and finally serving together.

TALKING TOGETHER

When we meet our neighbors, friends, colleagues, and companions at work, and when we meet on formalized occasions with those of other beliefs, our intent is to engage in dialogue with them. There is nothing mysterious about the word, "dialogue." It means simply a free, respectful, and mutually meaningful exchange between two or more persons or groups of persons. As we use the word, dialogue is not just a technique but a basic human activity whose significance is self-evident. Are any exchanges that are *not* free, respectful, and mutually meaningful desirable between people? Dialogue does not have to result in mutual agreement between the parties involved, but, if it is real, it will at least enable its participants to experience deepening interpersonal relationships. Understanding, trust, and openness will grow. When such an experience is lived together by people of different faiths, interfaith community is created.

Here are some suggestions to facilitate dialogue.

1. We should not expect that from the beginning of our encounter with people of other faiths we can plunge into a freely moving exchange of religious beliefs and convictions. It may not even be best to start with religion as the topic of conversation, unless of course, it comes up spontaneously. Also, given the fact that the other religious communities are much smaller in number than ours and much less well-known than ours, we should have the grace to listen for a long time to the others as they express their beliefs on their own terms. We should not assume that others will state their convictions in just the way we have read or heard. And let us not be overly eager to speak for ourselves at first. As we grow in trust, the freedom of both parties to speak will manifest itself. It may sur-

prise us sometimes to discover that our partners in dialogue know more about our faith than we do about theirs.

2. We should be humble enough to realize that all of us fall short of the ideals of our way of life, so we should beware of comparing our ideals with other peoples' actual practices. A colleague of mine used to warn people of what he called the "real you and the ideal me" syndrome in interreligious discussions. As we talk about our respective faith communities, we should be realistic enough to recognize that the Christian church also has some members who are uninstructed in their faith, who hold ideas about Christianity that are mixed with traditional ways, belonging more to folklore than to historic religion. Also the church has members who are actively concerned about issues like war and peace, the criminal justice system, health care, poverty, and women's rights, and so on. These contrast sharply with others who concentrate mainly on the personal life of faith, prayer, and devotion. Then there are the Fundamentalist Christians, those who advocate a back-to-basics approach to Christian beliefs and practices. As we take stock of the immense variety of outlook that exists among Christians, we can appreciate that Muslims, Jews, Buddhists, and those of other religions live with the same kinds of diversity within their own communities. We all have ideals, doctrinal and moral standards. But we understand and practice those ideals differently, so we should be humble and flexible dialogue partners.

3. Disagreement will inevitably occur, but we can prevent disagreement from leading to conflict.

To rob disagreement of its power to alienate would-be partners in dialogue, try asking questions again and again about the point of disagreement. Exploring it calmly with questions and answers may cause us to see that what started as a sharp disagreement is not such at all. It may be simply a different way of expressing oneself that is strange to the other party. Examples of such possible points of great divergence are how God's nature is understood in Islam, the function of law in Judaism, the meaning of idols in Hinduism, nonviolence in Jainism, and the unity of all religions in Baha'i faith. If, however, even after talking the matter through, we still disagree, we can in the interest of a larger goal—interfaith community—assume the moral burden of peaceful difference. In this connection, readers are invited to review the discussion of "Dealing with Differences" in chapter 3.

Formal occasions for dialogue present some difficulties and require careful preparation. Normally, participants should be well informed about the other faith before a dialogue takes place. Otherwise the occasion would be little more than a confrontation of positions. Information can be gained about the different faith positions through visits to places of worship and the ways suggested earlier in this chapter. These are a preparation for dialogue. Then when members of two or more religious groups meet to talk they can choose a common topic of interest and apply their respective points of view to that subject.

Ms. Kay Lindahl of the Alliance for Spiritual Community, described in chapter 4, has specialized in organizing and conducting interfaith dialogue groups. She stresses the need for a convener or a director, someone who is clearly recognized as overseeing the process of dialogue. This person could be chosen by representatives of the two or more groups who plan the occasion. Ms. Lindahl has also furnished an extensive list of possible subjects for dialogue. Here is a selection of those subjects (used with her permission):

- Single-issue topics: prayer, fear, freedom, love, family, community, friendship, justice, and service.
- How do you recognize your prejudices? How do you move beyond them?
- What are your core values? How do you nurture them?
- What do you do when faced with moral dilemmas? (Bring specific examples of how you resolved them.)
- How do you discern your unique talents/ gifts/contributions? How are you called to serve the world?
- What are miracles?
- What does your tradition teach about reconciliation? How do you practice reconciliation in this changing time where there is fear, anger, and violence?
- How is gratitude expressed in your life?
- What is the teaching of your tradition about violence? How do you deal with anger in yourself or when someone is using it against you?
- Is forgiveness essential in your spiritual/religious system?

These suggested topics are not directly theological, although they may have theological implications. Strictly theological dialogue is apt to be less successful than exchanges relating to practical issues of life and society, that is, unless the participants are equally competent in theology.

It is normal for people to join in prayer together, regardless of their particular religion, when there is a crisis—sickness, death, accident, or natural catastrophe. The form or manner of such prayer matters less than the common human cry of distress arising from a community in need. What people are doing in such a case is simply expressing together their awareness of a supreme being or power to whom or to which they refer with a will to show reverence and gratitude.

By contrast, when we turn to organized times of deliberate prayer together, the situation demands careful preparation. First of all, what is the occasion for such an event? Thanksgiving, Martin Luther King, Jr., Day, United Nations Day, a special concern such as world peace, or ecological conservation? Or the occasion simply to manifest the feeling of togetherness by a group otherwise separated by religion?

For such moments, some would recommend a kind of generic form, in which language, postures, and content express the lowest common denominator of those present. This formula is often used, but many find it to be too artificial and a violation of the integrity of those religious traditions represented in the group. This is an appropriate time to describe for readers a phenomenon that exists in our country that we might call the *interfaith movement*. In it there are interfaith churches, interfaith ministers, and interfaith seminaries serving those people who for one reason or another prefer not to align themselves with an established historical religious community. Leaders of this movement insist that they do not intend to supplant existing religions but rather to serve as a bridge to help people of faith to overcome the barriers of specific religious systems and to grow in communication with one another. While recognizing the good will and devotion of those in the interfaith movement, we discern ambiguity that makes it difficult for us to recommend it as a way to create interfaith community. It appears likely that, in spite of their statements to the contrary, they have created, in addition to the historic faiths, a new "way" which, at least for those who follow it, constitutes an alternative to existing religious communities.

And to return to the subject of prayer in interfaith community, this is precisely what is *not* recommended in such circumstances. Concerned believers do not need an alternative to their way of life but rather a clear manner to express themselves in the company of believers in other ways. So we suggest that when interfaith community manifests itself in a special meeting for prayer, the good will, common concern, and united purpose of such moments can best be expressed by participant groups when they use the language, forms, symbols, and thoughts that are native to them and mark their particular authenticity. If such is the case, then interfaith community in prayer really means members of different traditions praying alongside each other, not trying to pour their thoughts and feelings into an unreal interreligious mold. This, we feel, is an admirable manner for members of interfaith community to express their common humanity, the ties of religion that unite them, albeit in a general way, and their solidarity with others in facing the perplexities and ambiguities of life. Also those who listen and observe on such occasions gain valuable insight into the ways of prayer followed by different religions. (For a pertinent resource on prayer, see "Resources" at the end of this chapter.)

SERVING TOGETHER

We have seen that dialogue and prayer together present many difficulties given the great theological, cultural, and philosophical differences that separate the religions. It is likely that common service to one another and to a needy world is the best way to express our community feelings. Following are some practical suggestions for serving together:

Hate crimes are unfortunately committed against people of minority religions. So as a service to our people, we suggest that in interfaith community we make a deliberate effort to prevent religious hate crimes and to repair the damage done by them. Since 1985 there has been no attack on a house of worship in Rockford, Illinois. In that year the local Laotian Buddhist temple was attacked (United Methodist News Service, February 4, 2002). Immediately an interfaith council was formed and the Christian ministers paid a visit to the Buddhists, welcoming them to Rockford. So as believers seeking interfaith community we should be on the alert for situations in which people encounter misunderstanding or hostility. To ward off possible violent attacks, we should speak out against bigotry, racism, and intolerance. We should take a public stand, as an interfaith community, for tolerance, understanding, and more—a welcoming spirit toward minority religions among us. Other suggestions:

1. Send out messages of greeting and good will on the occasion of religious and cultural festivals celebrated by our interfaith partners.

2. Be alert to situations of misfortune, such as accidents, fires, and floods, in which people of other faiths are involved. Those seeking to create interfaith community can perhaps render service.

3. Give recommendations, where possible, to authorities in schools, hospitals, prisons, factories, and places of business and government having to do with features of certain cultures and religions with which most people are unfamiliar. Some of these are: dietary requirements, customs of dress, mingling of the sexes, religious instruction for children, and customs at childbirth and at death.

4. Join like-minded believers in coalitions and other associations to achieve common political and economic goals. Several examples of this kind of interfaith community were given in chapter 4.

5. Lend or rent church premises to other faith groups for their communal gatherings. It is likely that any such arrangement would be temporary, since most religious groups would not desire to be permanently identified with a church. Church buildings in the U.S. often have many rooms that are not used every day, so it should not be difficult to find a place to reserve for use by another religious community. The opportunity to render this service would also provide a good occasion for mutual learning about the faiths of the two groups involved. The sanctuary of a church would usually not be suitable for worship by several of the religions described in this book, since fixed pews would hinder the physical movements of the worshiper. Also, Christian symbols like the cross would make the sanctuary itself less desirable for use by others, such as Buddhists and Muslims.

6. Seek participation of other religious communities in local interfaith councils. Such groups can be significant expressions of interfaith community at the service of the people in general, provided they take the following precautions in their organization:

   • There will be full equality of membership, not simply in number of representatives or in financial participation. Equality produces the feeling of being truly represented in discussions and decisions, especially in the formulation of a constitution and determination of the objectives of the group.

   • Trust in and respect for each other must be fostered by perfect transparency of motives. Any harboring of ulterior motives, hidden agendas, and objectives will seriously weaken and possibly destroy interfaith relationships.

   • The cement of any interfaith organization is the pursuit of a common goal, something clearly defined and acceptable to all parties. We can suggest the overarching goal of mutual understanding in the pursuit of which more concrete, short-term goals might be agreed upon. Such objectives would conceivably put the group at the service of the larger community in forms of social, political, and economic actions. Another goal might be understanding through interfaith dialogue, following the guidelines given earlier in this chapter.

7. Join individuals from other faiths or any interfaith grouping where direct social service is administered in any of many forms: food and clothing distribution to the poor, help for children and mothers, tutoring for school children, etc.

8. Take part in cultural exchanges. These can be informal, such as visiting homes, sharing ethnic meals, and learning customs from other cultures. Or such exchanges can be more elaborate, such as holding a world religions fair, with exhibits prepared by different faiths, sacred music, dance performances, and dramatic presentations.

9. Offer English classes for new immigrants from other religions. This would be both a service to the community as a whole and a means for creating and strengthening interfaith community.

What Next?

Upon reading the preceding practical suggestions, I hope some readers will immediately find ways to participate in existing interfaith communities or else take steps to create or help create such communities. But not everyone is equally aware of the many religions in our midst. Some will recognize people in their towns and cities who belong to other religions. This will be especially true of teachers, social workers, government employees, doctors, nurses, salespeople, and others who work with the general public. These may find it relatively easy to develop personal friendships with persons of different faiths. For others with whom we may already be in touch, it remains for us to go deeper in our relationship with them as we discover our similar devotion to religion, albeit to different religions. These may include parents of our children's schoolmates, colleagues at work, neighbors, members of the same club, and partners in sports. Christians who understand this common participation in religion will have cleared the first hurdle in the way of responding to the challenge of a multifaith North American society. They will either know some of their fellow Americans of other religions or they will know where to look for them.

Other readers, however, before now may never have entertained the thought of interfaith communities and may be scarcely aware of the different religious groups around them. If this is your situation then you may well ask, "What can I do to be a part of an interfaith community, or what can my church or my women's group do?" The first thing to do is to identify people of other faiths. Rather than seeking out individuals who may be total strangers to you, it is better to start with a place of meeting or worship. The Jewish synagogue is usually well known. Other places like temples or mosques may not be so easily identifiable. Sometimes religious groups meet in private homes. Ask your pastor if he or she knows where the places of worship are located. The telephone book may provide some information (probably under the heading, "churches"). Also you may visit the website, http://www.pluralism.org. This is a service of the Pluralism Project at Harvard University, providing a vast database of religious centers throughout the U.S.

Next go with your pastor or with an officer of the group you represent to meet a leader or leaders of the other religious community. When you ask for an appointment with them, let them know that you have been studying about interfaith community. Ask if some members from the other religion would kindly come to your church and speak informally about their way of life and worship. If they accept your invitation, then discuss with the people at church certain principles of interfaith encounter, such as: the need to listen quietly to the others before speaking in a discussion period and to refrain from making superior claims for your faith and from trying to convert the other person. If refreshments are to be served, take care to know the dietary requirements of the other faith. Political issues should be avoided if possible, at least at this initial meeting.

You will find that your would-be partners in interfaith encounter are often eager to respond to such an invitation because they know how little most North Americans know about other religions. When they come to speak at your church they probably will not show much curiosity about your faith, but this does not matter at this stage. If the first meeting is successful, several possibilities for future action will reveal themselves. You will have formed friendships across religious lines and can nurture these friendships by subsequent contacts on an individual basis or in other gatherings.

A next step might be for the church or women's group to organize an open house at the church for friends, men, women, and children from the other community. Here again careful preparation is necessary. Always make clear that you are seeking to create interfaith community. No other motive is in view. To that end, instead of planning to speak about Christianity at the open house, discuss with your expected partners an agenda for the occasion. Suggest that, instead of having a formal speaker, one person from each religion be appointed to make brief presentations to make all those present feel at ease. Then the presenters, or one who has been appointed as convener, might pose questions to those present so as to stimulate conversation. One might ask:

"What do you see as a benefit from our meeting together this way in an interfaith gathering?"

"What do you think it might mean for all of us together to become an interfaith community?"

"How can we best continue our conversations together?"

"Is there any action or service that we can undertake together, even at this early stage, or should we wait until our relationship develops a little more?"

An initial open house might include refreshments, a time of getting better acquainted, and concluding words of thanks and appreciation for the occasion.

Another approach, either following the open house suggested above or in place of it, is to ask for a guided visit to the place of worship of the other religion in order to learn about the way services are conducted; the furnishings of the temple, mosque, or other space; and, of course, to deepen the friendships formed across religious lines.

In these first encounters you probably will not discuss weighty matters of theology or philosophy unless they come up spontaneously. But as other interfaith meetings materialize, the agenda can appropriately include such questions as marriage in the two faiths (including religiously mixed marriages), educating children in the faith, problems with the secular culture, religious festivals, business ethics, and the roles of men and women.

After these first initiatives, everything depends on the nature and quality of the relationships that develop. Other meetings may be organized. More dialogue may be in order. It may become obvious that together the participants in your interfaith experiment can render some service to the particular religious groups involved or to the larger community. At some point your group should examine the models of active interfaith community described in chapter 4 and decide if there is one or more of those that you can follow, or at least from which you can draw inspiration, as your interfaith community emerges to grace the life of your neighborhood, town, or city.

We have shown how creating interfaith community is an important way for Christians to witness to the universal love of God as revealed in Jesus Christ. In closing, we want to reemphasize that point by assuring readers that interacting with people of other faiths is not just a pleasant social and intellectual pursuit or only an adventure of the human spirit. For Christians, it is making ourselves accessible to serve wider segments of the human family than we have ever done before. And we do it in the company of the one who came "not to be served, but to serve, and to give his life a ransom for many" (Matthew 20:28). To quote from the policy statement of the National Council of Churches, "Interfaith Relations and the Churches":

Jesus comes among us as a servant. We too are given the opportunity to serve others, in response to God's love for us. In so doing, we will join with those of other religious traditions to serve the whole of God's creation. Through advocacy, education, direct services, and community development, we respond to the realities of a world in need. Our joining with others in such service can be an eloquent proclamation of what it means to be in Christ.

And finally, remember that the arena for our interfaith activities is the United States, an organization of human beings unique in the world. When we believers from various faiths create and maintain interfaith communities, talking peaceably with one another, finding our faith commitment not a hindrance but a help in bringing about social harmony and well-being, then we are embodying the ideals of the U.S. system. Our country is built on a social contract that unites a bewildering variety of classes, ethnicities, and cultures into a stable, dynamic structure called the United States of America. Religious people talking, praying, and serving together in interfaith community are, in the deepest conceivable way, truly Americans.

National Council of Churches, Interfaith Relations Office, 475 Riverside Drive, Room 870, New York, NY 10115, (212) 870-2560, www.ncccusa.org

The Presbyterian Church (U.S.A.) prepared a useful booklet, with study guide, called *Respectful Presence: An Understanding of Interfaith Prayer and Celebration from a Reformed Christian Perspective* (Presbyterian Distribution Service, 1-800-524-2612). This resource will be especially helpful in relating prayer to interfaith dialogue.

CREATING INTERFAITH COMMUNITY

A STUDY GUIDE

INTRODUCTION

As its general goal, this study guide seeks to place before the participants the twofold calling of the gospel in the context of communal living:

1) Christian community's calling to be neighbors.

2) Christian community's calling to be witnesses.

The overall goals of the study are to lead participants:

1) From fear of the "other" and self-centeredness to awareness.

2) From awareness to understanding and appreciation/valuing.

3) From appreciation/valuing to seeking commonalities.

4) From seeking commonalities to witnessing and creating interfaith communities.

The study guide also maps out particular goals for each of the four sessions in order to enable the readers to explore, analyze, reflect, and act in the light of the gospel to seek and work for the shalom of one's community, following the paths of one who came as "boundary-breaking God," even Jesus the Christ.

Session 1: What Is Interfaith?

1) To explore our theological and biblical basis to be neighbors in a religiously diverse community.

2) To raise awareness of our nation's religious diversity.

Session 2: Why Interfaith Community?

1) To understand the central teachings and beliefs of selected religions.

2) To analyze why it is imperative to be a neighbor in a religiously diverse community.

3) To seek commonalities and shared values in order to strive to live and work as neighbors.

1) To explore and share understandings of the Kingdom of God in the Bible.

2) To examine the key question in any of our interfaith relationships. What is it to be witnesses of Jesus the Christ and neighbors to people of different religious faiths?

3) To study various ways of building bridges to develop and strengthen the social fabric of one's community through interfaith relationships.

1) To explore different models of successful interfaith communities.

2) To resolve, as individuals and as a faith community, to develop action plans in order to be neighbors and witnesses, crossing barriers and creating an interfaith community.

Each session has key components such as worship, Scripture passages, and theological reflections in order to continue to understand one's core faith in Christ, one's own faith community, and the common task of working for an expanded inclusive interfaith community.

How and where do we build bridges between these two entities—(1) Christian faith community and (2) community? Envisioning this twofold task can be made easier through a metaphor or a diagram in an adult study context.

Therefore we resort to a *journey* metaphor. "Walking the walk" as a faith community as well as an interfaith community is a complex task for which we are called. But we are called to be border-crossers. "The boundary-breaking God," is going ahead of us.[1]

(Note: Quotations from the Bible are from the New Revised Standard Version unless otherwise indicated.)

Session

1

WHAT IS INTERFAITH?

Goals for this session:

(Facilitator writes these goals on newsprint before the class starts.)

1) To explore our theological and biblical basis to be neighbors in a religiously diverse community.

2) To raise awareness of our nation's religious diversity.

Things needed for participants for the four sessions:

The Bible; the basic text of the study book, *Creating Interfaith Communities,* by Marston Speight; several copies of *The United Methodist Hymnal*; *Global Praise 1;* and *Global Praise 2.*

Additional things needed for this session: Butcher paper (or dark cloth), newsprint, several nontoxic magic markers, 20 cue cards, ribbon or bright crepe, colored bond, construction paper.

Things to do before class starts:

1) Create a worship center.

2) Paste a long butcher paper, about ten feet long and four feet wide, across a wall horizontally.

The butcher paper represents a journey. Divide the paper horizontally into two parts, using a nontoxic magic marker. The lower part represents the Christian community. The upper part represents the general community. On the upper portion of the butcher paper, at the topmost part, write COMMUNITY. On the lower portion, at the bottommost part, write THE MEMBERS OF THE BODY OF CHRIST BEING NEIGHBORS AND WITNESSES.

(Option): Instead of butcher paper, you can create what is known as a "sticky wall." Take a lightweight piece of dark fabric, about five yards long and four feet wide. In a well-ventilated outdoor place, spray the cloth with a can of adhesive spray. You can buy it in art stores. When you do the spraying, take care that the spraying does not go beyond the piece of cloth. Get some help when you fold the cloth. This is your sticky cloth, which could be mounted on any long flat wall with masking tape. Divide the sticky wall into two parts horizontally with a ribbon or a brightly colored crepe paper. Write on a brightly colored bond paper, MEMBERS OF THE BODY OF CHRIST BEING NEIGHBORS AND WITNESSES, and stick it on the lower part of the sticky wall. Write COMMUNITY on brightly colored bond paper and stick it on the uppermost part of the sticky wall.

The sticky wall allows you to move the bond papers around quickly during class discussion, whereas such mobility is limited on butcher paper. The sticky wall can be used many times for educational purposes![2]

3) Prepare cue cards for the simulation exercise.

The suggested timings are only a reminder to keep the study on focus.

Opening prayer (2 minutes):

Infinite God made familiar to us in Jesus Christ, you call out each star in the sky by its name. Knowing God, you call us forth, each in your name, to step forth from the cozy familiarity of our homes and our friends into new and unfamiliar circumstances. Walk with us in this new way, in this unfamiliar path, as we set out to do this mission study. Gather our thoughts. Focus our attention. Fit us with your limitless vision as we seek to be neighbors and witnesses in obedience to your gospel. In Christ's name, Amen.

Group sings (5 minutes):

Pick any one of the numbers listed below from the hymnal or songbooks noted and sing all or only a couple of stanzas:

- *The United Methodist Hymnal,* #63, "Blessed Be the Name"
- *The United Methodist Hymnal,* #333, "I'm Goin' a Sing When the Spirit Says Sing"
- *Global Praise 1,* #5, "As your children, Lord"
- *Global Praise 1,* #36, "Jesu tawa pano (Jesus we are here)"
- *Global Praise 2,* #102, "The church is like a table"

Ground rules (5 minutes):

The facilitator enables the class to come up with a set of ground rules for the rest of the sessions. Write the ground rules on newsprint and post the list on the wall, separate from the butcher paper (sticky wall), where everyone can see it all the time. Even in the ground rules, on the first day itself, make it clear that no one person may dominate the discussion. Each person's idea should be listened to with respect, even though another may not agree with that idea.

Introduction of class members (15 minutes):

Participants make a *brief* introduction of themselves.

***Simulation exercise.* Insider/outsider during the time of Jesus (25 minutes):**

Make ready twenty cue cards with one of the following phrases written or typed on each card.

Distribute the cards at random to the participants in your class.

1) Women
2) Differently abled (lame, blind)
3) Women with ritual pollution (child birth, menstruation)
4) Persons who suffer from epilepsy and fits
5) The sick
6) Lepers and people with HIV/AIDS
7) Persons with various kinds of skin ailments, including skin cancer
8) Tax collectors (all those who work for the IRS)
9) Prostitutes
10) Servants
11) Slaves
12) Hog farmers (swineherders)
13) Sailors (seamen)
14) Peddlers of fruits and garlic
15) Gentiles
16) Those who follow the religious rituals regularly
17) Priests in the temple
18) Disciples of temple priests
19) Pharisees
20) Those who observe the minute regulations of purity

The facilitator says:

When I call out the following categories, please go to the door and stand by the door. *You are outsiders.* Now the following are 'bodily impure' people who were considered *outsiders* during Jesus' time. *(Reads aloud 1-7.)*

Now I am going to call out the next category of *outsiders*, who will join the first category of *outsiders* at the door. *(Reads aloud 8-14.)* During the days of Jesus, these were outsiders because their livelihood was considered polluting or sinful.

The third category of *outsiders* will join the first two categories of *outsiders,* that is, the "gentiles." *(Reads aloud 15.)* The rest (16-20) are *insiders.*

Now those who have cards and are still inside the room, please come to the front and stand facing the class. These are the people who are the *insiders.*[3] Read to the rest of us what is written on your cards, that is, 16-20. Others who are sitting inside the class will be *observers.*

Questions to ask the outsiders:

1) How does it feel to be an outsider?
2) What were some of your feelings when you were called to leave the room and stand at the door?
   a. How does it feel to be treated as an impure person?
   b. How does it feel to be treated as a gentile?

Questions to ask the insiders:

1) How does it feel to be part of an inner circle?
2) What are some of the privileges you have to give up in order to include the outsiders in your circle? Are you willing?

Questions to ask the observer:

1) Who made the rules of inclusion and exclusion?
2) What is it like to be an observer watching the acts of inclusion and exclusion?

To the insiders:

Do you want to include the outsiders? That means giving up your privileges.

To the outsiders:

Do you want to be included with the people who have so far treated you as outsiders? What does it take to be integrated with those who excluded you?

Read in small groups (10 minutes): Luke 4:18-19, Matthew 12:46-50, Mark 7:24-30.

Theological reflections (facilitator). Here are questions for reflection:

1. What is Jesus' vision of a new community?

2. How does Jesus define new relationship?

3. What is the key learning from the encounter between Jesus and the Syrophoenician woman?

First and foremost, *God loves all human beings.* God addresses all human beings as children of the same Creator. Such a claim makes all of our narrow categorizations irrelevant and parochial.

We Christians are being sent into the world with a clear mandate of communicating the message of the wholeness of God's concern, which forms the motive, the foundation, and the framework of our mission activities.

We are sent through Christ and empowered by the Holy Spirit to be a new community in Christ (John 17:18-19). This new community is not *of the world* but *in the world,* which clearly means the Christian community must integrate with the larger community in order to work as leaven. In other words, by maintaining our own identity, we find our task as peacemakers and reconcilers in the midst of challenges and conflicts. Through the action of God's community, all of God's creation is brought together (Ephesians 1:9-10).

Consequently, our ministries of mercy and human involvement as stated in Mark 10:45 are included in our integrating process and in our inextricable solidarity with the human community.

Read John 17:18-19, Ephesians 1:9-10 (5 minutes):

Questions for reflection:

1. What is God's will for the world today?

2. Who are the outsiders in your towns and larger community?

3. Who are some of the people considered "gentiles" or religious outsiders today by the Christian community?

Christian community needs to be a realistic, dynamic, and down-to-earth community to work as "salt of the earth" and "light of the world." The mission and ministry of the church are where the people of God are. If the church is to locate where the people of God are situated, the church's existence ought to be directly related to the concerns of the local community.

The church's concern and caring action for members of the community really demonstrates what the mission and ministry of the members of the body of Christ are all about. This "demonstration" needs to be more visible today than ever before. We often act only out of our personal or individual disposition, as we attempt to help our neighbors. Such an act is a subjective or an emotional or temporal act. It imposes our definition and assumption of the needs of others. But if we take seriously the biblical mandate to be neighbors, a larger community will be formed and a genuine neighborliness will be established.

Paul writes to the church in Ephesus that salvation is an act of reconciliation and creation of shalom. Consequently, Paul continues, the mission of the church becomes a mission of incorporation and creation of a reconciled community living as a sign of peaceful and peace-loving community in the world, striving to bring others into the community by crossing all human-made boundaries (Ephesians 2:11-22).

In short, the mission of the church is an act of the end-time believing community that is waiting for the appearance of Christ for a second time. This mission also means working in the meantime for the larger community!

Read Romans 1:20, II Timothy 2:10, II Corinthians 5:20 (5 minutes).

Questions for reflection:

1. How does God's plan of salvation for the whole of humanity have an impact on our lives?
2. What does it mean to be God's ambassador today?

Minority Christians living in other cultures increasingly strive to practice the bond of community as a prerequisite for peaceful living. Many have practiced it for centuries. On May 12, 2002, one of the authors had the opportunity to listen to the sermon preached in Mu En Memorial Church in Shanghai, China, by its Christian leadership. "Mu En" means "bathed in grace or showered by grace."

It is a 7,500-member church served by 200 lay workers, three elders, and two pastors. The sermon for the day stressed, "Showers of blessings of God are for everyone, not for Christians only." This sermon was accompanied by the old-fashioned hymn so dearly loved by many, "There Shall Be Showers of Blessing." These are old nuggets of truth and a plain old mission hymn. But ever-new interpretation is needed as the church tries to seek commonalities in order to interact with the community beyond its insular walls.

A Christian community cannot choose to remain an island of bliss bathed by God's grace. Blessings like rain and sunshine fall on everyone. In Matthew 5:45b, Jesus draws the attention of his listeners in his Sermon on the Mount to the Creator's benevolence.

The connecting bridge in our common journey as a faith community and an interfaith community is common humanity, *being children of the same creator.* "So God created humankind in [God's] image,/ in the image of God, [God] created them;/ male and female [God] created them" (Genesis 1:27). "From one ancestor [God] made all nations to inhabit the whole earth..." (Acts 17:26).

"Our first task in approaching another people, another culture, another religion is to take off our shoes, for the place we are approaching is holy. Else we may find ourselves treading on [human beings'] dreams. More seriously, we may forget that God was here before our arrival."(Clark Pinnock)[4]

We, children of God, are on a journey. We are all pilgrims. The notion that we have "arrived" is presumptuous. We must resist the temptation to use the gospel and God's revelation and action to Jesus Christ as a weapon against our neighbors whose history, culture, and faith traditions are different from ours.

"We must begin with the great reality made known to us in Jesus Christ, that God—the creator and sustainer of all that exists—is in his own triune being an ocean of infinite love overflowing to all his works in all creation and to all human beings." (Leslie Newbigin)[5]

As a people called United Methodists, we believe in the prevenient grace of God, the grace that exists in a culture before missionaries go there. The final aim of creating an interfaith community is not to bring all religions together or to find weakness and loopholes in each other's religious experiences and faith traditions. It is to know the will of God in our lives and for our common community. It is to understand each other better and to be more tolerant of one another. It is to eliminate fear and suspicion and to live in peace and harmony. It is to share our common concerns and inherent fears and find ways to address them.

Above all, it is to see each other in the mirror of another person's religion and culture and to correct our own limitations and sinfulness with the boundless compassion and limitless generosity of grace God has bestowed upon *all* of us.

(The facilitator draws the participants' attention to the butcher paper symbolizing the journey metaphor.) The class will journey together as the body of Christ learning ways and means to reach out to the community.

This is a twofold walk, if you will. (1) We seek to *walk the walk* as a faith community. (2) We find ways to *cross the boundaries* in order to cre-ate an interfaith community.

To demonstrate this visually, whenever there are insights of commonalities, biblical, theological, communal, and otherwise, anyone can draw a bridge between the paper's lower and upper portions, namely, Christian community and community.

For biblical and theological commonalities, use a specific color of magic marker. For common communal needs, use another color to draw bridges. For commonalities of social justice issues, use some other color.

The facilitator might begin by sketching a bridge between the lower and upper portions of the butcher paper and write COMMON CRE-ATOR or CHILDREN OF THE SAME CRE-ATOR. This bridge is a connecting link between MEMBERS OF THE BODY OF CHRIST in the lower portion of the butcher paper and THE COMMUNITY in the upper portion of it.

Overview (5 minutes):
The facilitator explains the "why" of the study, states the goals, and gives an overview of the study. In particular, the facilitator gives a brief summary of the introduction.

Individual Exercise—Identify religious symbols (5 minutes):

The facilitator distributes copies of Appendix A (page 130) to participants and asks them identify the key symbol of each religion.

Key symbols of selected religions practiced in the U.S., e.g., Christianity—Cross.
• Baha'ism
• Buddhism
• Hinduism
• Islam

- Jainism
- Judaism
- Sikhism
- Native American religions.

Small group reading exercise (20 minutes):

The facilitator organizes participants into eight small groups to read chapter 1. Assign a leader to each small group and allow 20 minutes for reading the passage. The small group leader facilitates the discussion in each group. Each group chooses a reporter to report to the whole group. The facilitator gives each group a light-colored construction paper (6 inches by 9 inches) so that each reporter can write on it. Make available a couple of nontoxic magic markers.

- Group 1 reads "Judaism."
- Group 2 reads "Islam."
- Group 3 reads "Baha'ism."
- Group 4 reads "Hinduism."
- Group 5 reads "Jainism."
- Group 6 reads "Sikhism."
- Group 7 reads "Buddhism."
- Group 8 reads "Native American Religions."

Discussion questions for each small group (do not take more than 20 minutes for reading and discussion):

1) What are the three key beliefs of the religion assigned to your group?

2) Draw the symbol of the religion on colored construction paper. The size of the symbol should not exceed 6" X 9". Across the symbol, write the core belief of the religion in one to three words.

Sharing with the total group (25 minutes):

Each group should take no more than three minutes to report. Report the three key beliefs to the total group.

Put the symbol that your group drew on the upper part of the butcher paper. While the reporter is putting her symbol on the butcher paper, the next person need not wait. The next group should start reporting.

The facilitator (to the total group—5 minutes):

1) What are the three key beliefs of Christian faith? Eliciting the three key beliefs, the facilitator has a cross cut out on a piece of construction paper and places it on the lower part of the butcher paper.

Key definitions:

Ecumenicity is different from interfaith. "Ecumenical" refers to the relation between and among various Christian denominations and traditions such as Presbyterians, Lutherans, United Methodists, etc.

"Interfaith" refers to meeting among different religions. Interfaith is a strategy, an objective. It is not a new faith.

Caution:

A different *denomination* within the Christian tradition is not a different *religion.* For example, Roman Catholicism is not a different religion. It is a different denomination.

Closing prayer (1 minute):

God of mission, you seek dialogue with us always everywhere. Help us to listen to you. Keep our eyes and ears, minds and souls open to the working of the Holy Spirit. Renew our flagging spirit. Refresh our inmost being. In the name of Jesus, we pray. Amen.

Reading assignment for session 2:

1) Finish reading chapters 1 and 2 in the study book.

2) Read the excerpt that follows from the United Methodist Resolution, "Called to be Neighbors and Witnesses: Guidelines for Interreligious Relationships," adopted in 1980 and revised and adopted in 2000. *(The Book of Resolutions of The United Methodist Church 2000, pp. 220-224)*

3) *Optional Research*—For more information on religious diversity in the U.S., maps showing the presence of various religious centers, etc., go to the website of Harvard University Pluralism Project: http://www.pluralism.org

Diana L. Eck, *On Common Ground: World Religions in America*. CD-ROM by Harvard Pluralism Project (New York: Columbia University Press, 1997). Phone 1-800-944-8648.

"America's New Religious Landscape." VHS video and discussion guide. Sixty-minute tape of selected clips from *Religion and Ethics News Weekly*. Price $15. Alban Books, www.alban.org

Nations of the world are growing increasingly interdependent politically and economically. The various world religious communities are also encountering each other in new ways. Religions of Asia and Africa are showing new life and power within their homelands and are spreading to other continents, creating multireligious societies, especially in western nations. New sects, cults, and ideologies are emerging and ancient traditions are receiving renewed attention. To an unprecedented degree, the wonders of the information age bring the world's rich religious diversity into our homes and communities.

The emergence of religiously diverse societies and the new dynamics in old religious communities have prompted many faith communities to reconsider how they relate to one another and to prevailing secular ideologies. This represents a great opportunity for learning and an enhanced understanding of our common concerns. Yet, there is also danger that religious tensions will lead to oppression of religious minorities and curtailment of religious freedom with real potential for armed conflict. At a time when worldwide problems of human suffering due to poverty, wars, and political oppression are so vast and pervasive that no one faith group can solve them, tensions between religious groups often prevent the level of cooperation needed to respond more adequately. As ancient religions demonstrate new life and power to speak to the deepest human concerns, Christians are pressed toward a deeper understanding of other faith traditions and a reexamination of their own claims to a global mission to all people.

What are the implications of this religiously diverse situation for Christian theology and ministry? What does it mean to be a faithful follower of and witness to Jesus Christ? What does it mean to affirm the Lordship of Jesus Christ in a religiously pluralistic world? Can we, of different faith traditions, live together as neighbors, or will diverse religious loyalties result in mutual antagonism and destruction? What are the resources United Methodist Christians bring for building constructive relationship between persons of different religions?

The United Methodist Church provides this statement as guidance to its members and congregations in facing these questions in their relations with persons who hold other faith perspectives.

Called to Be Neighbors

For some Christians, it may seem strange even to refer to "persons who hold other faith perspectives." Some are accustomed to calling them "non-Christians" or "nonbelievers." These attitudes may have developed out of confidence in the ultimate truth of our own faith perspective or from limited experience of and insensitivity to other traditions, to the truth they may contain, and the profound meaning and purpose they give to the lives of people. How, then, are we to relate to those who seem different from us religiously?

Scripture gives us many images of neighborliness which extends across conventional boundaries. In the Old Testament (Genesis 12), we find God challenging Abraham and Sarah to go and live among strangers. In the New Testament, Jesus breaks convention by speaking with the Samaritan woman at the well (John 4:6-30) and shows how she can be reached through dialogue. Speaking with a lawyer (Luke 10:25) Jesus reminds him that his neighbor, the one to whom he should show love and compassion, and from whom he may receive grace, may be a stranger. Today, our Lord's call to neighborliness (Luke 10:27) includes the "strangers" of other faith traditions who live in our towns and cities. It is not just that historical events have forced us together. Christianity itself impels us to love our neighbors and to seek to live in contact and mutually beneficial relationships, in community, with them.

What does it mean to be a neighbor? It means to meet other persons, to know them, to relate to them, to respect them, and to learn about their ways which may be quite different from our own. It means to create a sense of community in our neighborhoods, towns, and cities and to make them places in which the unique customs of each group can be expressed and their values protected. It means to create social structures in which there is justice for all and that everyone can participate in shaping their life together "in community." Each race or group of people is not only allowed to be who they are, but their way of life is also valued and given full expression.

Christians distinguish several meanings of "community." One definition expresses their relationships as members of one another in the body of Christ, the church, a people called together by Christ, a "communion of saints" who work toward the reign of God. A broader definition points to the relationship that is shared with others in the wider human community, where Christians are concerned with peace, justice, and reconciliation for all people. Other faiths also have their understanding of "community." The vision of a "worldwide community of communities" commends itself to many Christians as a way of being together with persons of different religious convictions in a pluralistic world.

Called to Be Witnesses

Within this religiously diverse community, Christians, trusting in Jesus Christ for their salvation, are called to witness to him as Lord to all people (Acts 1:8). We witness to our Lord through words which tell of his grace, through deeds of service and social change that demonstrate his love, and through our life together in the Christian community, exhibiting God's power to heal, reconcile, and unite.

When Jesus issued his famous missionary mandate, "Go therefore and make disciples of all nations" (Matthew 28:19), the Greek word [for "go"] is *poreuthentes.* This literally means "to depart, to leave, to cross boundaries." Thus, a witness to Jesus Christ is one who can bridge boundaries, be they geographic, sociological, racial, or cultural. The gospels tell story after story of Jesus crossing boundaries and reaching to outsiders, drawing them into his circle. As disciples of Jesus, our outreach draws upon the gospel call to be even more than neighbors. We are to proclaim and witness to the God who has bound humanity together to care for one another, regardless of the differences between us.

As relationships with persons of other faith communities deepen, Christians discover how often our witness has been unneighborly, how much we have talked and how little we have listened, and how our insensitive and unappreciative approaches have alienated sincere truth seekers and persons who already have strong faith commitments. We become aware that we frequently communicate attitudes of superiority regarding our own faith, thereby perpetuating walls and hostilities between us as human beings. These can only restrict Christian witness.

As United Methodist Christians reflect anew on our faith and seek guidance in our witness to and encounter with our new neighbors, we discover that God who has acted in Jesus Christ for the salvation of the whole world, is also Creator of all humankind, the "one God and Father of all, who is Lord of all, works through all, and all in all" (Ephesians 4:6 TEV). Here Christians confront a profound mystery—the awareness of God who is related to all creation and at work in the whole of it, and the experience of God who has acted redemptively for the whole creation in Jesus Christ. Christians witness to God in Jesus Christ in the confidence that here all people can find salvation and in the trust that because of what we know of God in Jesus, God deals graciously and lovingly with all people everywhere.

Session

2

WHY INTERFAITH COMMUNITY?

Goals for this session:

(Facilitator writes these goals on newsprint before the class starts.)

1) To understand the central teachings and beliefs of selected religions.

2) To analyze why it is imperative to be a neighbor in a religiously diverse community.

3) To seek commonalities and shared values in order to strive to live and work as neighbors.

Things needed for participants:

1) An old tattered jacket or coat. Write SCAPE-COAT on a piece of paper and pin it across the coat. If that is not possible, draw the figure of an old coat on large construction paper or newsprint and cut it in the shape of a coat. Write across it in big bold letters SCAPECOAT.

2) A pad of adhesive notes.

3) The study book, hymnals, Bibles.

Prior research required: The facilitator is encouraged to familiarize herself/himself with the different ways in which the cross, the major Christian symbol, is used to promote hate and hate crimes. A good resource is *When Hate Comes to Town: A Handbook of Effective Community Responses* (Center for Democratic Renewal, 3rd ed., 2001-2002), pp. 135-137. Available from Service Center, stock number 1412, price $10. Phone 1-800-305-9857. Fax 1-513-761-3722.

Additional prior research recommended for facilitator: raise consciousness about how hate groups use the internet. Visit www.stormfront.org. Become familiar with websites that challenge hate. The Simon Wiesenthal Center established the Task Force Against Hate in 1991. It tracks hate on the internet. Visit http://www.wiesenthal. com/taskforce/index.cfm. Visit also the United Against Hate website at http://www.unitedagainsthate.org/main.cfm.

Opening prayer (2 minutes):

Eternal God, we claim to be made in your image. But we often fail to practice Christ-likeness as our true identity. Rather, we remain satisfied with acquired identities that fetch us advantages and privileges. Yet you summon us to recover our identity as your children, created in your image, in order to glorify your name, sanctify our lives, and live in harmony. Equip us for this morning, for this new study. Renew Christ-likeness in us, seeds sown in humiliation to be raised in glory. Amen.

Group sings (5 minutes):

• From *The United Methodist Hymnal:* #560, "Help Us Accept Each Other"
• #428, "For the Healing of the Nations"
• *Global Praise 1,* #51, "O many people of all lands"

Litany: Our Father in Heaven (3 minutes):

Leader: If we have hallowed you as "Our Father in heaven," and have cut ourselves off from you and each other,
If we have prayed for your Kingdom to come and have not worked for it,

All: ***Lord, have mercy upon us. Christ, have mercy upon us.***

Leader: If we have prayed for your will to be done and have schemed and acted in our own ways,
If we have prayed for our daily bread and succumbed to the economics of consumerism at the expense of our neighbors,

All: ***Lord, have mercy upon us. Christ, have mercy upon us.***

Leader: If we have sought forgiveness from you for our sins, and have not had the grace to forgive our neighbor,
If we have prayed to overcome temptation, and have not trusted in the strength of your love,

All: ***Lord, have mercy upon us. Christ, have mercy upon us.***

Leader: If we have prayed for deliverance from evil and have not risked an unpopular witness to stand against structures of evil and iniquity,
If we have prayed for your Kingdom, power, and glory, and have manufactured our own gods,

All: ***Lord, have mercy upon us. Christ, have mercy upon us.***

Words of peace:

God gives strength to the least of God's saints. God gives strength to set aside every weight and sin that clings so closely. God helps us walk the walk and cross boundaries. God even helps us run with perseverance the race that is set before us, looking to Jesus, the pioneer and perfecter of our faith. Amen.

Theological reflection:

The facilitator summarizes in a few sentences of her or his own words the following Scripture passage. Break into small groups to read and discuss the passage.

Read in small groups: Acts 17:24-28.

Questions for reflection (7 minutes):

1. Among all of God's creation, human beings are the foremost, since they are created in God's image. If so, why do some Christians claim themselves to be superior to others?

2. Can you describe the face of God? God's true self?

3. Why do we need to create interfaith communities?

The New Testament speaks of the universality of truth and divine revelation. The Apostle Paul declared to the religious Greeks of his time, who were gentiles, that God "has not left himself without a witness" (Acts 14:17). The Epistle to the Hebrews says that God had spoken to our forebears in many and various ways by the prophets; and in the last days, he has spoken to us through God's Son, Jesus Christ (Hebrews 1:1-2).

God reveals God's self to all inquiring minds and searching hearts. We are all children of one God. We are all made in the image of God (Genesis 1:26). We are all members of the divine family. God has made of one blood all nations to dwell on the face of the earth (Acts 17:26).

Even though people of other religions practice other beliefs and are rooted in other faiths, other cultures, other histories, other traditions, and other civilizations with long distinctive pasts, many live and work in our neighborhood, shop in our town, and live like the rest of us do. Their children go to schools with our children and play with ours.

They fight crime and violence and work for a safer community. They have family values, community standards, national goals, and aspire for global peace just like all of us. Most are honest, hardworking, law-abiding, and tax-paying citizens just like any of us. Most of all, they have longings, desires, and aspirations just like all of us. As a community involved in God's mission, we Christians must join hands with people of other faiths to remove fear, drive away hatred, and put out any divisive spirit that may come in the form of bigotry, racism, and violence.

In the past, broadly speaking, people of other faiths lived far away from us in another part of the world, and the relationship between Christians and people of other faiths largely took place under the umbrella of economic might, military power, technological superiority, and political dominance. The relationship has always been, as John Hick says, "downwards" not "sideways." Now that these people of other faiths are right in our neighborhood, we encounter them every day in a variety of settings. Hence it is a

> **The God who made the world and everything in it, he who is Lord of heaven and earth, does not live in shrines made by human hands. . . . From one ancestor he made all nations to inhabit the whole earth, and he allotted the times of their existence and the boundaries of the places where they would live, so that they would search for God and perhaps grope for him and find him—though indeed he is not far from each one of us. For "In him we live and move and have our being" . . . "For we too are his offspring." Act 17:24–28**

necessity to know and understand them as community members in order to have a peaceful coexistence.

Read I Peter 3:15.

Questions for reflection (5 minutes):

1. Interfaith communities can also open our eyes to the way others view us. Others can serve as mirrors for us to know who we are and how we are perceived. For instance, people of other faiths are often baffled at how Christians who claim to be followers of Jesus Christ, the divine self-revelation, often practice arrogance and hatred toward outsiders.

2. How can Christians who claim to be followers of one God be divided into denominations? If Christians are not in agreement with each other in their beliefs and practices regarding the oneness and service of humanity, how can they bring agreement among religions of the world for its common good?

Many non-Christians in the U.S. live in fear and suspicion because of racial hatred and cultural intolerance. They huddle together and find safety in numbers. In such a context, people of other faiths can remind us that we need to repent and be born anew everyday just as much as they do. Our encounter with those communities will teach us how we are viewed and why we have become a problem for others. They can teach us what our own faith looks like when it is not practiced the way it is supposed to.

Our encounter with people of other faiths will help us understand how our culture, politics, economy, art, ideas, and narrow patriotism have infiltrated the gospel of Jesus Christ and how deeply clouded they can make the message of love and reconciliation offered through Christ, the prince of peace.

Moreover, ignorance and misunderstanding of the adherents of other religions, with their different cultural practices and faith traditions, will generate hatred and prejudice, which eventually will result in a broken community and hostile humanity.

Read Psalm 137:4 and have small group discussion (4 minutes):

1. How do you suppose the followers of other religions interpret this passage?

2. Mahatma Gandhi once said, "Christians are the worst disciples. They do not follow their guru (master) and his teachings?" Is he right?

Finally, the Christian message can never be separated from social change and prophetic utterances. It can never be isolated from poverty and exploitation. If Christian mission is to succeed, it has to go to the place where the people of God, *all* people of God, reside. Social changes and community reforms can be realized only in cooperation with all the people in a community, regardless of their backgrounds.

Stanley Samartha, a former staff member of the World Council of Churches, says Christian mission is "God's continuing activity through the spirit to mend the brokenness of creation, to overcome the fragmentation of humanity, and to heal the rift between humanity, nature, and God."[6] Above all, the Great Commandment, as indicated by Jesus, tells us to love God as well as our neighbor (Mark 12:29-31).

Drawing bridges:

At the end of the theological reflection, the facilitator draws bridges between Christian community and community at large on the butcher paper and writes across the bridges core theological and missional principles. Examples: MADE IN GOD'S IMAGE (Genesis 1:26), LOVE GOD (Mark 12:30), LOVE NEIGHBOR (Mark 12:31). Completion of previous day's assignment on chapters 1 and 2 (10 minutes): Those small groups previously unable to give their reports may do so. Small group discussion on resolution "Called to be neighbors and witnesses" (10 minutes):

The facilitator divides the class into two halves. In groups of three, half the class reads the first four paragraphs and "Called to Be Neighbors" from *The Book of Resolutions* printed in this guide at the end of the suggestions for session 1. The second half of the class reads the first four paragraphs and "Called to Be Witnesses" in the resolution. The groups discuss the following questions respectively.

Questions to answer—first half of the class:

1) Who is your neighbor?

2) Define Christian community.

3) Define larger community.

Questions to answer—other half of the class:

1) What does it mean to be a witness?

2) What is referred to as the "profound mystery"?

3) What is a Christian witness according to the assigned reading?

Simulation exercise: border-closing versus border-crossing (15 minutes):

Put up the SCAPECOAT on a prominent place. Distribute to the class a couple of sheets from the adhesive notes. Ask participants to write down some of the biases and discriminations people undergo because of their religion. Write down also the stereotypes and name-calling associated with people of other religions. Allow three minutes for writing. Then ask participants to read out the answers to the entire class and stick the answers on to the SCAPECOAT.[7]

Symbols of the cross used for hate crimes (5 minutes):

The facilitator refers to "Symbols of Hate" found on pages 135-137 of *When Hate Comes to Town: A Handbook of Effective Community Responses.*

Small group discussion—Chapter 2, "Why Interfaith Community?" from the study book for this course, *Creating Interfaith Community* (20 minutes). Divide the total group into five small groups. Divide the chapter into small chunks for reading among these five groups. *These small groups will be permanent groups for the rest of the sessions.* Read and discuss questions given below.

Discussion questions:

Each group chooses a leader to facilitate the discussion and a reporter to report to the total group. Each group picks up a piece of newsprint for writing its key points in discussion. Each reporter should take no more than four minutes to report to the total group.

1) Summarize key ideas in the reading assigned to your group.

2) Why is creating interfaith community in your town/region more important than ever in the aftermath of the September 11, 2001, tragedy?

3) On your newsprint, draw a historical timeline starting with September 11, 2001. The title of

the historical timeline is "Reviewing the past two years." What are the major events that happened in your church community and the larger community in the past two years in the wake of September 11, 2001? List media coverage, strategies adopted to address the tragedy of September 11, the faith community's response, the larger community's response, etc.

Example:

September 11, 2001—World reacts with horror to the events; people watch media coverage with a mixture of fascination and revulsion.

September 12 to December 2001—People give generously to aid victims of the tragedy; U.S. begins attack on the Taliban; many people are arrested in the U.S. on suspicion.

January to April 2002—People react in different ways to increased airport security; financial scandals of Enron and other corporations distract and depress; some terrorists are arrested.

4) Looking at the historical timeline you have created, pick up things that can be called "bridge-building efforts" (positive things) and "bridge-closing efforts" (negative things).

Reporting to the total group (20 minutes):

After reporting orally, each group reporter draws bridges across the butcher paper. In instances of bridge-closing efforts, the reporter draws a broken bridge across the butcher paper. In the interest of time, such drawings should be done when one of the groups members finds time during lunch or dinner break.

How to monitor hate crimes (5 minutes):

1) The facilitator summarizes pages 42-49 in *When Hate Comes to Town* in his/her response to the discussion. Also make copies of the list of organizations that participants should contact when there are hate crimes in their communities. See Appendix B, pages 131-134 of this Study Guide.

2) (a) Check whether your state has a hate crime law, and (b) who the protected groups are. There is increasing concern among faith and human rights groups about hate crimes aimed at people who are perceived to be followers of Islam or who look like people from the Middle Eastern region.

(c) Be a data collector and help track hate crimes and violence nationwide for the General Board of Global Ministries. Scan newspapers for articles on hate crimes and clip them with name, date, and other information, and send them to:

The Women's Division
General Board of Global Ministries
475 Riverside Drive, Rm. 1502
New York, NY 10115-0050.
Attn: Ministries in the Midst of Hate and Violence

(d) Continue to visit GBGM websites: http://gbgm-umc.org/advance/church-burnings, http://gbgm-umc.org/programs/antihate, http://gbgm-umc.org/umw/anti-hate.

Exercise of being bridge-builders and bridge-closers:

The facilitator should invite participants to stick their written ideas and suggestions for being bridge-builders as well as confessions of being bridge-closers across the butcher paper during their free time in the School of Mission.

Closing worship: Sing hymn #560, "Help Us Accept Each Other," from The United Methodist Hymnal. The facilitator may lead a one-sentence prayer.

Assignment for next session:

1) Read chapters 3 and 4 from the study book, *Creating Interfaith Community.*

2) Read the excerpt given below from the United Methodist resolution on "Called to be Neighbors and Witnesses" (*The Book of Resolutions 2000,* pp. 224-227). Familiarize yourself with two kinds of dialogue: (a) What is dialogue as a way to be neighbors? (b) What is dialogue as a way of witness?

3) See video "Not In My Town," especially the segment on religious intolerance (optional for next session).

4) *Also optional for the next session:* Role play by one of the participants in the class on a teenage Muslim girl wearing her head covering (*hijab*, pronounced he-jab). One of the participants could do a role play based on a real story recorded in an essay by a teenage Muslim girl in St. Mary's Episcopal School in Memphis, Tennessee. The essay could be downloaded from your learning center or any public library, if you do not have personal access to the internet: http://www.pluralism.org/affiliates/allman/essay.php?from=affil_alman

Dialogue—A Way to Be Neighbors

"Dialogue" is the word which has come to signify an approach to persons of other faith communities which takes seriously both the call to witness and the command to love and be neighbors. To be engaged in dialogue is to see witnessing and neighborliness as interrelated activities. Rather than a one-sided address, dialogue combines witnessing with listening. It is the intentional engagement with persons who hold other faith perspectives for purposes of mutual understanding, cooperation, and transformation.

"Dialogue" may be as informal as a conversation in the marketplace or as formal as the leader of one religious group explaining to others its belief or worship life. Dialogue is more than an individual or academic enterprise. It also involves groups or communities of people holding different convictions who reach out to one another. This community orientation gives a practical bent to interreligious dialogue.

In dialogue, one individual or group may seek relationship with another in order to expose misunderstandings and stereotypes and to break down barriers that separate and create hostility and conflict. Ethnic or religious communities may approach each other in dialogue in order to resolve particular problems or to listen to foster cooperation in dealing with a local, national, or even global situation of human suffering. At its deepest level, dialogue is both learning about and sharing our faith through its stories and images. Each partner learns from the rich store of wisdom of the other, and each expresses his or her own deepest conviction in the faith that it has truth worth sharing with the other.

Through dialogue with persons of other faith communities, new insights are received regarding God's activity in the world today, the divine purpose for humankind as a whole, and the place of the Christian community within these purposes. It is also a common experience for Christians to feel the need to express their own faith with greater clarity. We trust in the Holy Spirit to make known new and different insights through such encounters.

Even though Jews, Christians and Muslims share the same covenant, in many of our cities and towns we continue to live as strangers to each other. A positive foundation from which to connect with persons in other faith communities is recognition of some of the gifts they bring to the human community. For instance, through Judaism, Christians can connect to the covenantal faithfulness of God; Islam illustrates the joy of life lived in obedience to God's will; the spiritualities of indigenous peoples encourage a deep reverence for God's natural creation; Buddhism offers contemplative ways to connect to the divine; and Hinduism in its varieties brings the gift of tolerance. Engaging in dialogue with positive expectation offers the possibility of sharing mutually beneficial spiritual gifts as well as overcoming past hostilities.

Dialogue frequently has been misunderstood. Some see it as limited to the commonalities that exist between different religious traditions. It is important to discern and explore those commonalities and to utilize them to strengthen relationships. But there is more! Dialogue offers to both partners the opportunity of enriching their own faith through the wisdom of the other. In the process it helps overcome the deep mistrust, hatred, hostility, and conflict that characterize so many intercultural and interreligious traditions. Each religious community asserts that its faith offers a way to resolve conflict in positive ways and has resources for building community among diverse peoples. Dialogue seeks to provide an environment which allows space for differences, builds on the positive affirmations of each faith, and brings them into relationship with each other.

Dialogue—A Way to Witness

The only precondition for dialogue—sometimes a challenging one—is a true willingness to enter a relationship of mutual acceptance, openness, and respect. Effective dialogue requires that both partners have deep convictions about life, faith, and salvation. True dialogue requires that Christians not suspend their fundamental convictions concerning the truth of the gospel, but enter into dialogue with personal commitment to Jesus Christ and with the desire to witness to that faith. Effective dialogue also requires that Christians be truly open to persons of other faith communities, to their convictions about life, truth, and salvation and to their witness, as others also feel called to witness to their faith and teachings about the meaning of life. Engagement in dialogue is a form of Christian ministry.

Is not this urge to witness an obstacle to interreligious dialogue? It often has been, but it need not be. Where there is listening as well as speaking, openness and respect as well as concern to influence, there is dialogue and witness. Indeed, dialogue at its most profound level is an exchange of witness. Participants share with each other their perceptions of the meaning of life, of ultimate reality, salvation and hope, and the resources of their faith for enabling community. In genuine "dialogue," we "witness and are witnessed to." The most effective dialogue takes place when both sides really do care that the other hear, understand, and receive the other's wisdom. Part of our witness is our openness to hearing the witness of the other.

Dialogue at these depths holds great promise. Long-cherished convictions may be modified by the encounter with others. Misunderstanding may be clarified, potential hostilities reconciled, and new insights regarding one's own faith may emerge in contrast to that of another. The depths of another's faith may be so disclosed that its power and attractiveness are experienced. Dialogue is a demanding process, requiring thorough understanding of one's own faith and clear articulation of it to the other person. It asks that we "translate" our perspectives to one another with integrity, that we have the patience and attentiveness to discern what meaning words and images have for the other persons as well as ourselves.

Dialogue is not a betrayal of witness. Dialogue and witness are wrongly placed in opposition to each other. They need each other. Dialogue creates relationships of mutual understanding, openness, and respect. Witness presses dialogue to the deepest convictions about life, death, and hope.

Many persons of other faiths are suspicious that dialogue is a new and more subtle tool for conversion. In some ways this is inevitable, since Christians do want others to learn of and receive the truth and grace we know in Jesus Christ. The difference between dialogue and other forms of witness is that it is a context for learning from the other the truth and wisdom of the other faith as well as sharing with the other the truth and wisdom of our own. We leave to the Holy Spirit the outcome of our mutual openness. Our concern is to be obedient to our own call to witness and to follow the imperative to be loving and neighborly to persons of other faith communities. In dialogue, these deeply held truths encounter each other in witness and love, so that greater wisdom and greater understanding of truth may emerge which benefit all parties in the dialogue. As we exhibit courtesy, reverence, and respect and become neighbors, fears of each other are allayed, and the Holy Spirit works within these relationships.

Session

3

THE "HOW" OF INTERFAITH

Goals for this session
(Facilitator writes these goals on newsprint before the class starts.):

1) To explore and share understandings of the kingdom of God in the Bible.

2) To examine the key question in any of our interfaith relationships. That is, what is it to be witnesses of Jesus the Christ and neighbors to people of different religious faiths?

3) To study various ways of building bridges to develop and strengthen the social fabric of one's community through interfaith relationships.

Things needed: study book, Bibles, *The United Methodist Hymnal, Global Praise 1,* newsprint, pencils, paper, Band-Aids, a bandage for an arm sling, ribbon or fabric wide enough to be written on, construction paper, a bookstand, and a small basket.

Things to do before the session starts:

1) The facilitator should write on three separate sheets of newsprint a very brief summary of "pluralism," "inclusivism," and "exclusivism" given below and put them in a place on the wall where everyone can see.

Pluralism:

People of other religions are saved in and through their own faiths. Hence they need not be evangelized or converted. Christian mission has to encourage them to use the best part of their religious teachings in order for them to become better adherents of their own faiths and serve humanity.

Inclusivism:

God sent Jesus Christ to die for all people (II Corinthians 5:14) and hence God's spirit brings salvation to all people regardless of their religious affiliation. Those who hold such a conviction also view that the grace of Christ operates in and through other faith traditions whether the adherents of these faiths know and acknowledge Christ or not. Hence, they argue, the followers of other religions do not necessarily have to become Christians, and evangelization is not necessary.

Exclusivism:

God has uniquely revealed God's self in the person of Jesus Christ, and hence other faiths of the world do not have the means to redeem their adherents. These faiths merely serve as preparation for the gospel, just as Judaism prepared the way for the coming of the messiah in the person of Jesus Christ. Hence the gospel must be preached to them.

2) Worship center:

On the altar, right in the center, place a cross. This is an acknowledgment of God's fullness of revelation in Jesus Christ. Write on a piece of ribbon in magic markers FULLNESS OF REVELATION IN CHRIST and put it across the cross. Place an open Bible at the foot of the cross.

In a corner of the altar, place a bookstand and write on a piece of ribbon or construction paper, GOD'S HIDDENNESS. This could be otherwise done on a piece of fabric spread across the altar. The writing could be done on the hanging portion of the cloth in front for everyone to see.

Keep a basket in another corner of the altar. If any one of the participants is in doubt, he or she can write on a piece of paper the following incomplete sentence: "For me, the hiddenness of God is . . . ." This phrase, placed at the foot of a cross, symbolizes one's acknowledgment that there are things that humans cannot understand and only the Holy Spirit can teach us in our journey of faith as Christians. Participants can write on a piece of paper things which they cannot fully understand in the context of interfaith relations and place them in the basket.

Anyone can pick up one such piece of writing and pray about it and share his or her insights in the class. The facilitator should be able to guide the process prayerfully with biblical references and interfaith models.

Additional resource needed for distribution:

The section on encounter with other faiths from the free brochure, "Partnership in God's Mission: Theology of Mission Statement," pp. 14-15, published by the General Board of Global Ministries. Free copies of the entire brochure (stock #5003) are available from the Service Center.

Additional resource for the facilitator:

Familiarize yourself with the three positions of Christians toward people of other faiths. See Glory Dharmaraj's "Dialogue" in *Concepts of Mission,* pp. 26-28. (Available from Service Center, English version, stock #2820; Spanish #2992; Korean #2993; $6 each).

Class sings (3 minutes):

Global Praise 1, #25, "For sake of life"

The United Methodist Hymnal, #114, "Many Gifts, One Spirit"

Invocation from Mechthild of Magdeburg,

Germany, 13th century (2 minutes)

The United Methodist Hymnal, #104, "Praising God of Many Names"

Litany, The Word in Love with Dialogue (2 minutes):

Leader: In the beginning was the Word.

All: From eternity to eternity is the Word.

Leader: The Word seeking dialogue,

All: The Word pining for utterance.

Leader: For human dialogue,

All: For flesh and blood conversation.

Leader: The Word became dialogue in Jesus.

All: The Word became communication in Christ.

Leader: Incarnate Word,

All: In immaculate birth.

Leader: Cutting loose our monologues,

All: Driving us into dialogue.

Leader: The whole creation in dialogue,

All: Day and night in dialogue.

Leader: You and I in dialogue, Lord,

All: Therefore, "they" and "us" in dialogue.

Leader: Community-seeking God,

All: Monologue-breaking God,

Leader: Nudge us into fits of laughter and strength of community.

All: Draw us from the shadow lands of things that hold us back.

Leader: God who breathed life into our nostrils,

All: Breathe love into our community-making efforts.

Leader: Help us to live the Word,

All: The Word forever in love with dialogue, even Jesus the Christ. Amen.

Theological reflections:

Read the whole chapter or selected verses of Acts 10 (3 minutes).

The facilitator should summarize key concepts from the following reflections in two minutes.

When we read Acts 10, we come across the story of a Roman centurion, Cornelius. The narration tells us that God heard the prayers of Cornelius even while he was a gentile. God's ways are mysterious, sometimes even hidden. Acts 10:4 can be an instance of God's hiddenness.

The notion of God's hiddenness, rooted in biblical texts, was emphasized by Martin Luther during the Reformation. In a different context, Luther talks about the unknowability of God apart from God's own complete disclosure.

God's revelation came to us in its fullness through Jesus Christ. That is God's disclosure. However, there are things we, as human beings, cannot fully understand unless God continues to nudge us and reveal to us our own limited grasp of God. God listening to Cornelius's prayer while the latter was *not yet* a Christian (Acts 10:4) can be an instance of the hiddenness of God. Consider also verse 35: "[I]n every nation anyone who fears him and does what is right is acceptable to him."

Questions for theological reflection in small groups (10 minutes):

1. The Conference on World Mission Evangelism of the World Council of Churches, held in 1999 at Salvador, Brazil, noted that "Christians prayerfully and humbly ask: To what extent may [the adherents of] other religions be acknowledged as being expressions of God's mercy and grace found in Christ? At what points do these expressions appear to run

counter to God's fullness, life, and love in Christ?"

2. Read Romans 11:28-33, I Timothy 2:3-4, and John 10:16 and discuss whether God's plan for salvation includes those who are "outside of the fold."

In the Christian faith journey, in the context of interfaith relations, a Christian often stretches her or his hand to other Christians who believe in the full revelation of God in Christ. At the same time, a Christian also stretches his or her other hand to peoples of God who believe in other faiths. A backward and forward dance movement, if you will, is carried out by the people of God for the sake of all God's peoples.

A Christian dances in the light of Jesus Christ. A Christian is also willing to dance in darkness because God also dwells in darkness (I Kings 8:12). These are the forward and backward strokes, if you will, of one's dance with Christ, who has revealed God fully to us, and also with God, whose "hiddenness" is still a mystery to us. In this dance, the leader is the Holy Spirit who may lead us away from the traditional dance floor, the church, to the household of God, the larger community.

So let us march simultaneously in the light of Jesus Christ as well as in the darkness of God in our journey of creating interfaith communities. Let us sing one of the best-loved African songs, which perhaps can capture the twofold movement: "We are marching, We are marching, O we are marching in the light of God." May we add one more line to this favorite? "We are marching, We are marching, O we are marching in the darkness of God" (as well). The Holy Spirit is the leader of this marching. Trust the Holy Spirit leading the beloved community step by step in order to build God's kingdom.

Dialogue and the Kingdom of God

Christian faith tells us that Christ died for the world, that salvation offered to every human being who commits her or his life to Jesus Christ. Nonetheless, some of the unresolved questions are: How is salvation offered to the millions who live outside the boundaries of the Christian church? What is the role of world religions in bringing salvation to their followers? It is not easy to answer these questions in this single session.

The purpose of this part of the session is to learn how to live as Christians in the midst of religious pluralism, including building a nonviolent community.

Encountering people of other faiths helps us understand the values and gifts of our own beliefs so that we may not absorb our faith with mindless assimilation. Such an encounter challenges us to rethink our position and role in a pluralistic world.

We need to realize that people of other faiths are not always interested in our religious history. They may not pay much attention to our theological beliefs. Rather, they are usually more concerned about our relationships with them— our act of being neighbors with them. In other words, people of other faiths may not be interested in our "theology," but they are very much interested in what Kosuke Koyama calls "neighborology." Koyama means the way we are neighbors with people of other faiths. After all, our "neighborology" is the point of contact between Christians and people of other faiths.

Our neighborology, acts of being neighbors, should give us an open mind and listening ears to hear what others are saying. Only if we engage in a dialogue or conversation will we be able to create a shared community, work toward restoration of shalom, and go about living as a harmonious community, which is the goal of God's kingdom.

During his conversation with Christian missionaries, Mahatma Gandhi once said Christianity should be like a rose flower "which does not preach but exudes its fragrance in peace and makes its presence known in silence."[8]

The future of our faith should not be a mere preservation of ancient traditions, but rather the fulfillment of Christ's commandment and the establishment of a kingdom community through communal participation and interfaith dialogue.

Dialogue

The focus of interreligious dialogue needs to be the kingdom of God more than the church. Dialogue helps us discern how God uses even others and other ways to build God's kingdom.

Building up the kingdom is a wider cosmic reality. In the power of the Spirit, all are called to it in various ways known to God alone. In this constructive task, some may be challenged more particularly by Jesus and his gospel without hearing the call to discipleship and community (example: Mahatma Gandhi).

We need to engage in dialogue because doing so dispels misunderstandings and moves us towards collaboration with others in defense of common human values. Dialogue also allows us to share with others our God-given resources. Such sharing will enhance our prophetic roles for the betterment of our common humanity. Finally, dialogue may provide us with a common moral and spiritual foundation to build a better world.

If we make the kingdom of God the focus of our dialogue, that would and could embrace all the major social activities of mission.

Change of focus from the local church to the kingdom of God will not lead us to ignore the call to discipleship. The gospel can hardly transform society unless it is effectively made present by a community of called people who are committed to and involved in this historical process.

The demand to be in dialogue with people of other faiths and to collaborate in building up the kingdom of God does not in any way reduce the responsibility to witness to one's faith. The collaboration that is called for is not based on the least common denominator but on mutual and collective enrichment. Such collaboration respects the freedom of each one to respond to God's call in whichever way it comes to him or her.

Interfaith communities centered on the kingdom of God will be active and dynamic. They are future-oriented. They are rooted in reality and history. Most of all they are integrative and holistic, since they build up a new humanity.

Interfaith communities centered on the kingdom of God will lead the world and all peoples to their fulfillment. For there is a need for all religions to collaborate in the cause of humanity and to work for the attainment and preservation of human rights, such as the struggle to eliminate hunger, poverty, ignorance, persecution, discrimination, and every form of enslavement of the human spirit.

Interfaith communities centered on the

kingdom of God will treat all religious groups with equal honor and promote pluralist religious societies as a source of richness contributing to mutual growth rather than a source of tension.

> For the sake of life our God became an infant.
> For the sake of life he lived and died for all.
> For the sake of life the time of God is constant.
> The kingdom is at hand—for the sake of life.

Previous day's assignment: Discussion of chapter 3 (10 minutes).

Previous day's assignment: Discussion of reading assignment on pp. 224-227 of _The Book of Resolutions 2000_ (10 minutes).

• What is dialogue as a way to be neighbors?

• What is dialogue as a way of witness?

Selected three positions of Christians towards other religions.

Lecture method on _Concepts of Mission,_ pp. 26-27 (5 minutes).

Church and Interfaith, a skit (20 minutes):

Cast (11 volunteers): An announcer, a moderator, Dr. Plural, Dr. Exclude, Dr. Include, Ms. Ailing Giant (who represents the church), and five callers. Names should be written in bold letters on bond paper and pinned onto the front of the shirts of the cast. The rest of the class will be the studio audience.

The cast members are seated on chairs in a panel. Ms. Ailing Giant is seated in a reclining chair. She could use a chair to sit in and another on which to put up her feet. She has Band-Aids all over her body. One of her arms is in a sling. Five callers will stand at the various corners of the room. The announcer stands up to introduce the cast and then sits down.

**Announcer:** This is United Methodist SOS Telecast. I am Vivian Walters. This morning's panel discussion is on the topic, "What should a Christian's position be toward other religions?" Let me introduce you to the moderator of the panel, Ms. Veteran UMW. _(Turning to the studio audience.)_ The panelists you see, seated to the right and left of the moderator, are Dr. Plural, Dr. Exclude, and Dr. Include. Seated slightly away from them in a reclining position is their mother, Ms. Ailing Giant, otherwise known as the Mamma Church. She says she is quite sore from the lifelong rifts on her body because of disunity in her family. She wants to be left alone, unless she wants to say a few words in between. I honor her request. _(Turning to the studio audience, which is the group.)_ Now welcome Ms. Ailing Giant and her children, Dr. Plural, Dr. Include, Dr. Exclude, and our moderator, Ms. Veteran UMW. _(Turning to the panelists.)_ Thanks for taking time to be with us. The topic for this Sunday morning's show is: "What should a Christian's position be toward other religions?" Now I hand over the mike to the moderator.

**Moderator:** Thank you, Vivian. Good morning, studio audience and audience out there. As you heard, the topic for our morning show is "What should a Christian's position be towards other religions?" At the end of the panel discussion, our studio will take a couple of calls, including overseas calls. Because of the nature of the topic and the ten-second sound bite culture we all live in, I invite the panelists to be brief. Now our experts will present their arguments. Dr. Plural.

**Dr. Plural:** I believe in the equality of _all_ religions. There are many roads to the same destination that is *God*. I do not see why we should consider Christianity to be the only way to salvation. People of other religions are being saved in and through their own religions. *No one* religion can claim *absolute truth* about its understanding of God.

Moderator: Thank you Dr. Plural. Now Dr. Exclude.

Dr. Exclude: God has revealed God's self in a special and unique way in the person of Jesus Christ. Other faiths *do not* have the means of *salvation* to redeem their followers. We *must* preach the gospel to them. *The gospel is the one and only truth.*

Moderator: Thank you. Now Dr. Include will present his view.

Dr. Include: I believe God sent Jesus Christ to die for all people. The grace of God in Christ is operating in other religions also. People in these religions may not know or acknowledge that it is the activity of Jesus Christ. *That does not mean* they are not saved.

Moderator: Now that you have all stated your basic positions, you are given an opportunity to quote an example or narrate a brief instance to prove your point.

Dr. Plural: The one I like most is the story of the blind men and the elephant. *(Turning to the other two on the panel.)* Remember the story Mamma told us when we were small? Six blind men went to see an elephant. One got hold of the elephant's trunk and said, "The elephant is like a rope." The other got hold of the elephant's leg and said, "It is like a tree." Another one felt one of its ears and said, "The elephant is like a fan." The abdomen looked like a wall to another. My point is, each one is right, brothers and sisters. No one has the total vision to grasp the Divine Reality.

Dr. Exclude: But Mamma also told us that precisely for that reason Jesus came and opened our blind eyes. You have a selective memory of our Mamma's story. Someone described religion as a human being grasping God. But I believe that *God grasps us.* That is the difference between your interpretation and mine. That is my point too. Blind men grasping an elephant is one thing. The elephant taking hold of those blind men is another thing. God taking hold of us in Christ in a tender yet firm way and opening our eyes is *the story of Christian faith*. God *reveals* God's self to us in Jesus Christ.

Dr. Include: With due respect to Mamma, I should say Mamma never took wide travels when we were very young. She had to look after us. Only after we grew up did Mamma have a chance to visit other places and got exposed to other religions.

Ms. Ailing Giant: I am sick and tired of the church meetings where people often talk and talk and pass resolution after resolution and do nothing about them. I am for diversity of opinions, but what I hate is any talk which does not lead to action but sits on a piece of paper. That is why I was not very sure whether I should even show up here. I tell my children here just two things. I am aging. Children, love one another. *Love God and love your neighbor.*

Dr. Exclude: "Good fences make good neighbors."

Dr. Plural: Remove fences. They are all imaginary anyway.

Dr. Include: In reality, most of our neighbors *do have* fences and want to maintain them. But find some *common ground* where our gates could open into and let people in. Recognize places where fences *are* needed and where they *are not* needed. My position is *be open, but be not open on all sides.*

Moderator: We have heard your positions toward people of other religions. Sum up your position toward other faiths in one sentence.

Dr. Plural: All people know the truth through various revelations given to them.

Dr. Exclude: Only I know the unique truth because of the revelation given to me in Jesus Christ.

Dr. Include: I know the unique truth given to me in Jesus Christ, but others may not know that it is the same revealer of truth who is talking to them as well.

Moderator: That is one *long* sentence. Thank you. Now we open this panel to the callers. Keep it short. We are running out of time.

Caller 1: My name is Ms. Evangelical from Chicago, Illinois. You guys on the panel, "Do you weep for the souls?"

Caller 2: My name is Ms. Conciliar from Tulsa, Oklahoma. You guys on the panel, "Do you weep for the poor?"

Ms. Ailing Giant: I want to respond to this question. Look at me, folks. Look at the bandaged and divided body of Christ. Because of your fights over the centuries, I am in these heavy bandages. When will you stop fighting? Go. Read the gospel. Do not divide and fence up the gospel.

Caller 3: My name is Ms. Two-Thirds World. First I want to ask whether Mamma Church has any girls. Only boys seem to be representing most of the theologies on interfaith. Second, remember the Two-Thirds World Christians, who mostly live in the midst of other religions. Our churches are growing by leaps and bounds. You guys, when will you come up with a theology of neighbor and neighborhood? Western Christianity has produced so much theology about God, often overwhelming to the readers. Come up with a simple theology for Christians in a dominant culture relating to people of other faiths who constitute minorities. We will continue to live our calling as minority Christians in a majority non-Christian culture. In fact, we have learned to be tolerant of our neighbors over centuries in the midst of adversities and joys.

South-to-South Missionary: My name is South-to-South Missionary in Bangladesh. Shed your dominant approach. Repent of the past colonization and imperial attitude which disfigured the face of Christ. Once you do that, do not be ashamed to witness to the gospel in private and public places.

Ms. Ailing Giant: That is what I have been saying recently. *Christianize Christianity.* This is what one of my well-known children in Europe also is saying. *Christianize Christianity.* I think he wants to say, "Be more like Christ." That son of mine often cannot say things simply.

Caller from Europe: My name is Hans Küng [pronounced King]. I am the one who cannot say things simply. I too have my bandages. The church also inflicts wounds on her children, by the way. My own Mamma Church did it to me. But I love my own church, anyway. *Yes, Christianize Christianity.* But I would also like for you to put up a poster I have sent to you. *It is simple,* by the way:

"No peace among the nations without peace among religions.

No peace among religions without dialogue between the religions."

Moderator: Thank you callers from within and outside the U.S. We are coming to the close of the show. Let me summarize today's panel on Christianity and other religions in two questions.

Dr. Plural, Dr. Exclude, and Dr. Include: Questions again? We want simple answers.

Moderator (looking at the panelists.): That is the problem with our church today—demanding pat answers.

Ms. Ailing Giant: Yes, that is my children's constant problem.

Moderator (turning to the studio audience):
The two following questions will be asked of you over and over again in this century. How you address them will heal or divide your Mamma Church. You, studio audience, will continue to discuss this as you leave the studio. One is Jesus' question, "Who do you say that I am?" (Matthew 16:15) The second, to paraphrase Jesus, is "Who is your neighbor?" (Luke 10:36) *Go and live these questions in the household of God, your community.* You have heard the experts speak on the topic. Now I leave this for you to decide individually. In the meantime, *do not forget to love God and love your neighbor, two basic commandments in a nutshell. Take good care of your mamma, the church.*

Announcer: This is your announcer, Vivian Walters. For all of us here at UM SOS Telecast, thank you for being with us. Goodbye.

Total group discussion (15 minutes):

1) What are the merits and/or limitations of the three positions towards people of other faiths?

Individual activity—Know Your Faith (write on a piece of paper, 5 minutes):

1) Read Matthew 16:13-17.

2) What is your personal response to Jesus' question, "Who do you say that I am?"

3) What are the unique parts of the Christian faith?

4) Share responses with the entire groups.

Small group activity—Discussion of chapter 4 (10 minutes):

Question: Divide yourselves into four subgroups and read the passages assigned to you below. Lift up models of interfaith bridge-building. Report to the total group. Continue to draw bridges on the butcher paper as you discover new ways of relating to people of other faiths.

Group I: First three paragraphs of "Some Active Interfaith Communities" and "Talking Together" from the study book.

Group II: "Praying Together."

Group III: "Serving Together."

Group IV: "Community in Several Forms."

Two Kinds of Christianity—A Reading (10 minutes):

The facilitator should introduce the following reading. As two people read, ask the class to listen to the conversation and identify bridge-closing instances and bridge-building instances within practices of Christian faith.

Triumphalist Christianity versus Suffering Christianity

Reader 1: I am a Christian.

Reader 2: I am a Christian.

Reader 1: My name is Triumphalist.

Reader 2: My name is Suffering.

Reader 1: I am Success Christianity.

Reader 2: I am perceived as Failure Christianity.

Reader 1: I am otherwise called Imperial Christianity.

Reader 2: I am otherwise called Servanthood Christianity.

Reader 1: I ride on the back of sword and might.

Reader 2: I am carried by the power of the gospel.

Reader 1: I wear the glory of Emperor Constantine and the crown of colonization down through the centuries.

Reader 2: I wear the thorns of the cross-bearing Servant and am ashamed of the use of military might in my name to conquer and colonize peoples.

Reader 1: I am the Spirit of the Crusaders.

Reader 2: I am the Spirit of the Crucified.

Reader 1: I see the cross from above.

Reader 2: I see the cross from below.

Reader 1: From the conqueror's point of view.

Reader 2: From the conquered point of view.

Reader 1: My empire stretches from the West to the East.

Reader 2: "My Kingdom is not of this world."

Reader 1: Who are you then?

Reader 2: I am a Christian called Crucified Spirit. Who are you?

Reader 1: I am a Christian called Crusading Spirit. Do I know you? You are *not* a Christian. Are you?

Reader 2: We parted company long ago when Emperor Constantine declared Christianity the official religion in the 4th century. *You may not recognize me.*

Reader 1: (lifting up his or her collar) I am the majority religion here.

Reader 2: I am the Way of the Cross. Minority Christianity here.

Reader 1: I am the best-known face of Christianity here in town.

Reader 2: I am the least-known face of Christianity here.

Reader 1: Bigger crowds will follow only a conquering model of Christianity. Triumphalist Christianity. Don't you see?

Reader 2: Discerning people may be few. But I know they make a bold commitment to Christ as Suffering Servant.

Reader 1: You know what? That is the dumbest way to act. To follow the suffering model. Go and "imperialize" yourself. You can *sell* yourself better in this town.

Reader 2: You know what? You look like the tempter who tempted Jesus to fall down and worship him. I tell you something. Christ is *not for sale.* Go and "Christianize" yourself.

Reader 1: A Christian to Christianize oneself? The best joke I have ever heard!

Reader 2: A Christ-like Christianity is the best thing that can ever happen to Christianity in this town.

Reader 1: Christianity in emperor's style. That is the way to go.

Reader 2: Christianity as the Way of the Cross and Resurrection. That is the way to go.

Reader 1: There are two kinds of Christianity—Success Christianity and Failure Christianity.

Reader 2: Jesus said, "Unless I fail, my work will be useless."

Reader 1: Follow me. I will make you successful.

Reader 2: Follow me. I will make you faithful.

Personal meditation—Making Christianity Christ-like (10 minutes):

Secular Gods versus Christ-like Christianity

(1) Triumphalist Christianity has all along worked hand in hand with false gods like imperialism, militarism, racial superiority, and unbridled free trade at the expense of true Christianity. We are called to a twin calling: (a) Being responsible citizens for a true democracy in the only superpower country and (b) Being responsible Christians in a church in the U.S. that is fast losing its membership but whose voice of witness in the public square is vital for making a difference in the world. Answer the following questions yourself and find out whether your twin tasks, being responsible Christians and being responsible citizens, collide in your daily living.

(a) Identify some of the secular gods of today, e.g., mammon.

(b) Can one be a Christian and worship false gods offered by a secularized society?

(b) Is God *"God"* in my life or is God just a "god" in my life?

(c) In what ways can I demonstrate my Christian stance against the secular gods in our culture?

(d) How can I exemplify my Christ-like spirit in the dailiness of discipleship?

Closing thought: *"The greatest rival of the gospel is not Buddhism or Islam, or any other great faith but secularism."* (Rufus Jones, a Quaker, in the International Missionary Council of 1928 in Jerusalem)

Jesus Christ never founded a religion. Therefore Christianity is more than a religion. It is the person of Jesus the Christ who exemplified a new way of life. Come and walk it. Sing it.

Closing hymn: *The United Methodist Hymnal,* #432, "Jesu, Jesu."

In the second stanza, you might substitute relevant words for your own community.

Example:

Neighbors are Muslims and Sikhs, neighbors are Hindus and/ Jews, Neighbors are near and far away./ Jesu, Jesu, fill us with your love, show/ us how to serve the neighbors we have from you.

Assignment for discussion in the next session:

1) Individual assignment

(a) What is it to be saved? How do I understand "sin" and "salvation" as a Christian?

(b) How can I deepen my faith in Christ while I am about the task of building bridges as interfaith community?

(c) Read chapter 5 in the study book.

(d) Underline key words and key passages in the following excerpt. What particular position does the General Board of Global Ministries take, according to the passage given below?

(a) Pluralist

(b) Exclusivist

(c) Inclusivist

(d) Other (identify)

"Mission in a new age will increasingly encounter persons of other religious faiths. Many religions of the world are experiencing a resurgence of influence and fervor. Engagement and encounter, conversation and cooperation with persons of other religious faiths provide a unique opportunity for complete and enriching Christians witness.

"In the presence of persons of other faiths, the church in mission is challenged to be clear in word and deed about the message of salvation from God in Christ which it has received and with which it is entrusted. In dialogue with persons of other faiths, Christian faith is enriched and deepened in understanding and articulation. In encounter with persons of other faiths, the new life in Christ which the church seeks to embody is put to the test of living witness and demonstration. In dialogue and encounter with persons of other religious faiths, Christians hear God's word echoed through other traditions, while also bearing witness to the unique revelation of God in Christ which has been given to the church. United Methodist mission partners engaged in witness with persons of other religious faiths draw upon the assurance of the prevenient grace of God, remembering that the saving work of God is within the church and beyond."

("Encounter with Other Faiths," from "Partnership in God's Mission: Theology of Mission Statement," General Board of Global Ministries, pp.14-15. Free brochure available from the Service Center.)

2) Small group assignment

Each group will come up with *one* model with concrete action plans to build bridges of interfaith relations. Some examples are as follows:

Celebrating children's Sabbath in one's community; using a variety of prayers from different faith traditions; working on common issues like public school education, adult literacy, English for interested new immigrants, refugee resettlement, peace, conflict resolution, violence (including media violence), environment, poverty, living wages, women's Social Security, women's equal pay, farm workers' rights, sweatshops, child labor, public service radio announcements for an interfaith affirmation of living in unity amid diversity. Present your action plans for *one model* with projected time frames of implementation.

Session

4

WHO WILL GO?

Goals for this session (Facilitator writes these goals on newsprint before the class starts.):

1) To explore different models of successful interfaith communities.

2) To resolve, as individuals and as a faith community, to develop action plans in order to be neighbors and witnesses, crossing barriers and creating an interfaith community.

Things needed by the participants: the study book, *The United Methodist Hymnal, Global Praise 1 and 2,* a handbell, strings or light rope, two scarves, paper plates, napkins, grapes or an orange, eyeglasses.

Things to do before class:

For the commitment worship at the end, make ready four to five paper plates with some table grapes or one orange for each of the plates. Some paper napkins would be helpful.

Class sings (3 minutes):

Global Praise 2, #124, "My heaven"

Global Praise 2, #119, "There are tables in our city"

The United Methodist Hymnal, #431, "Let There Be Peace on Earth" and #593, "Here I Am, Lord"

Prayer:

Jesus, our go-between, thank you for bridging the gulf between God and our human self. You call each one of us this morning to be go-betweens for your sake. What a task, Lord! But the truth is you believe we can be go-betweens. Personally, I even begin to like the new name, Lord—a go-between. But teach us how to be one. We are eager. We are waiting for your Holy Spirit to open new ways for us to be in mission. Amen.

Litany—We Want to See Jesus (10 minutes):

Here is an account of a go-between in John 12:20-23. Listen to the role played by Philip, one of the disciples of Jesus, when a group of Greeks, who were considered gentiles at the time of Jesus, comes and says to Philip, "Sir, we want to see Jesus." (The facilitator reads aloud John 12:20-23.)

(Selected participants read the parts. The rest of the group acts as Greek chorus.)

Voice 1: We have heard peasants and philosophers. We have known teachers and preachers.

Greek Chorus: We want to *see* Jesus.

Voice 2: We have watched the sunrise and sunset; felt the rain and dryness; known birth and death; weddings and funerals.

Chorus: But we want to *see* Jesus.

Voice 1: We have known private fears and public terrors; personal tears and collective laughter.

Chorus: And we want to *see* Jesus.

Voice 2: We have known ups and downs; buying and selling; manual barter and electronic transfer.

Chorus: But we want to *see* Jesus.

Voice 1: We have seen doctors and medicine men; shamans and wisewomen.

Chorus: But we want to *see* Jesus.

Voice 2: We have seen technological marvels and military might; height of drama and depth of poetry.

Chorus: But we want to *see* Jesus.

Voice 1: We have seen chapels and steeples; campuses and retreats.

Chorus: But we want to *see* Jesus.

Voice 2: We have heard the noise of religions and voices of humans.

Chorus: But we want to *see* Jesus.

Voice 1: We have heard storytellers and myth-makers; trend-setters and image-brokers.

Chorus: But we want to *see* Jesus.

Voice 2: We are seekers and searchers. We have journeyed within and journeyed without.

Chorus: But we want to *see* Jesus.

Voice 1: "You have given your goods to feed the poor."

Voice 2: "You have given your bodies to be burned."

Chorus: "We also ask for love. Give us *friends.*"[9] Give us neighbors. Give us go-betweens because *we want to see Jesus.*

Theological reflections:

Read Isaiah 61:1-2 and Luke 4:18-19 (7 minutes).

These are parallel passages. Jesus reads the Hebrew Scripture in the synagogue in his home town. The narrator of the Luke passage leaves out a significant component of this reading—the element of vengeance.

Questions for reflection:

1. To what extent has our culture influenced the interpretation of the gospel?

2. To what extent have other forms of spirituality, such as yoga, meditation, etc., influenced our forms of worship and faith?

The test of living out one's Christian faith in communal living today is one's ability to contribute to the elimination of vengeance and violence. Our real point of reference with people of other faiths today is not the unity of religions or uniformity of practices but the pain of being torn apart. Hence the urgency of the creation of a peaceful and just community.

The need to associate ourselves with our shared human community, which is made up of people who have different religious practices, may not be mediated by our membership of collective identities, such as nationalities, race, religion, and culture. We can best learn about other religions by realizing that God is working outside the Christian community.

We can learn to understand the worldview of the people of other faiths that have deep spiritual and value systems. We can accept there are other ways of conceiving the world and arranging one's life on earth. We can acknowledge that people of other faiths also have ways of relating that are spiritual, humane, kind, just, inclusive, and community-oriented. We can be receptive for new insights even if religious differences may seem irreconcilable. Religions differ; their searches differ.

As in race relations, some people tend to deny the differences that exist among religions. We have heard people say, with all good intention, to people of color, "I am blind to your color. I do not see your color." However beautiful the color-blind ideal may be, many people of color actually want their white brothers and sisters to "see" their color difference, acknowledge the difference, and then go beyond it to build an inclusive community. To say that similarities and differences are not relevant assumes that all are in a similar situation.

There are some irreducible differences in religious beliefs when it comes to concepts of sin and salvation. As for Christians, there are internal differences in defining mission, missions, evangelism, salvation, etc.

In spite of differences in religious beliefs, the urgency for living as neighbors and exercising common humanity does not change. The calling of the people of God to address social justice issues in order to make a liveable world for all God's peoples does not change. God's promise and offer of a new earth and new heaven in Isaiah 65:17-25 is an alternative vision for God's people living amidst all God's peoples.

For instance, Judaism admonishes, "You shall love your neighbor as yourself" (Leviticus 19:18). "What is hateful to you, do not do to your fellow men. That is the entire Law, all the rest is commentary" (The Talmud, Shabbat, 31*a*). Christian Scripture tells us, "You shall love your neighbor as yourself" (Matthew 19:19*b*). Hinduism states, "This is the sum of all true righteous: deal with others as thou wouldst thyself be dealt by. Do nothing to thy neighbor which thou wouldst not have him do to thee after" (Mahabharata). Islam says, "No one of you is a believer until he desires for his brother that which he desires for himself" (Sunnah). Buddhism states, "Hurt not others in ways that you yourself would find hurtful" (Udana-Varga 5:18).

Know your own faith traditions and let your experience with your neighbor's spirituality challenge and transform you to a higher level of communal living in order to "exude fragrance." Listen and understand the messages of other religions as their followers witness to them, even as we witness to our faith in Christ. Recognize that God has not limited God's witness to that of Christians alone (Acts 10).

In his book, *The Impossible Vocation:*

Ministry in the Mean Time (Cambridge: Cowley, 1988), John Snow says that the goal of our ministry is "the construction of a world in which Christian symbols should make sense." The greatest symbol people of other religions see daily is the human symbol. Let them see who you are and whom you represent as a Christian. The Bible says Jesus Christ is the primordial sacrament, absolutely necessary and uniquely revealed for human beings' encounter with God. Hence the Protestant churches believe and practice two sacraments, baptism and holy communion, in commemoration of Christ's death and resurrection. These sacraments are shared only in and among the believers. However, there is another sacrament, a third sacrament, which Christ offers to people of other faiths—you and me, the disciples of Christ!

In the final analysis, creating an interfaith community depends upon the response Christians give to the people around them, through their words and deeds, to Jesus' question, "But who do you say that I am?" (Matthew 16:15).

A Skit—Gender and Interfaith (20 minutes):
Cast: A detective with make-believe detective glasses (which can be simply a set of eyeglasses), four readers, a volunteer representing Womanhood, and a person who rings a bell every 12 seconds in mild tones.

The volunteer sits on a chair facing the class. She is sad. The four readers are standing around her. Each reader has a rope or a scarf in her hand. Print the following identification names on bond papers and pin them across the chests of each of the readers. Reader 1: CHRISTIANITY; Reader 2: JUDAISM; Reader 3: ISLAM; Reader 4: HINDUISM. A bell ringer stands in a far-off corner of the room, and when the detective gives the signal, she starts ringing the bell every 12 seconds throughout the skit.

Detective: I want you to look at this WOMAN. She sits here unable to distinguish the voice of patriarchal culture from the voice of the sacred scriptures. That is because often people have used scripture texts to keep her in a subordinate role and even silence her. She does not even know that there are passages from the same scriptures which could be used to liberate her, heal her, and empower her. The following conversations will show you how various scriptures are used and abused for the liberation and the subordination of women respectively.

At the same time, I want you to listen to what is going on in an average woman's life. Every twelve seconds in the United States, a woman is battered. The bell which you will hear symbolize violence against women.

A woman's woundedness may come from the same source as her empowerment. Let us listen to some passages from various sacred Scriptures whose interpretations have inflicted wounds on women in their respective religious traditions. *(Bell ringer starts ringing the bell, mildly but steadily, from the farthest corner, every 12 seconds, to show that a woman is battered every 12 seconds in our country.)*

Reader 1: *(Goes to the person at the chair and speaks to her.)* "[W]omen should be silent in the churches. For they are not permitted to speak, but should be subordinate (I Corinthians 14:34). The guidelines for the activities and qualifications of women's service in the church are laid down in I Timothy 2:9-15 and I Timothy 5:9. Let me read a couple of verses. "Let a woman learn in silence with full submission. I permit no woman to teach or to have authority over a man; she is to keep silent. For Adam was formed first, then Eve; and Adam was not deceived, but the woman was deceived and became a transgressor." *I am a Bible-believing Christian. (Reader 1 goes to the woman at the chair and binds her mouth with a scarf.)*

Reader 2: That reference to Adam and Eve which you have just read is from the Torah, our sacred text. We value the creation story that tells us in Genesis 2:18-23 that God created Adam first and Eve second. Therefore, male superiority over woman is a God-ordained condition. I agree with my Christian friend. Our Talmud also describes women in one place as "greedy, eavesdroppers, lazy, and jealous." In fact one of the Hebrew words for husband is "ba'al," which also means *master.*[11] I believe husbands are masters of their wives. *(Goes and ties the hands of the woman in the chair.)*

Reader 3: I believe in the Koran, the Word of God. Though our sacred text does *not* say that woman is created after man, many followers of Islam were influenced by these particular Christian and Jewish interpretations of the creation story. This story is useful to keep a woman submissive to her husband. There is another passage which is used to keep women under men in our culture. This is a passage from the Koran quoted against any form of birth control. I quote:

Your wives are

As a tilth [tilled earth] unto you

So approach your tilth

When or how you will (Sura 2:223).

This is a permission sanctioned by Allah to husbands. They can have sexual relations with their wives whenever they choose. The right to impregnate is the husband's. The wife does not have any say in it.[12] *(Reader 3 goes and ties the eyes of the woman in the chair with another scarf.)*

Reader 4: I am a Hindu woman. One of the oldest texts in our religion, The Code of Manu, written almost 4,000 years ago, says:

"When a woman is a child, she should be submissive to her father. When she is married, she should be submissive to her husband. When a widow, she should be submissive to her sons. She should never be independent." *(Walking to the chair.)* This religious text has influenced men and women for many centuries. A good one to keep women submissive to men. Just think of it. Someone thought about it 4,000 years ago! *(Ties the feet of the woman in the chair.)*

Detective: *(Rushes to the scene.)* Stop it. Stop it. Will you?

Readers 1-4: *(They rush to the chair and block the detective's passage to the chair.)* Who are you to stop us?

Detective: I am Detective Interfaith. *(Pointing at the readers.)* You have quoted 4,000-year-old to 400-year-old Scriptures. You are all accomplices in interpreting your texts to your advantage. Everyone of you, Christian, Jewish, Muslim, and Hindu, shackles this woman with your religious interpretive chains. I see some strange commonality among you, when it comes to the treatment of this woman. *(Pointing to the woman at the chair.)*

You, you have been sitting in this chair for thousands of years without talking back to these people who have been putting shackles all over your body. I pity the woman who cannot even get angry, when injustices are meted out to her by person after person. *(Turning to the group.)* See this woman? I call her "diminished humanity." Whatever is done to diminish the full potential of a woman diminishes the rest of us, men as well as women. I have used my detective glasses *(She straightens her eyeglasses.)* to find out liberative passages from the same sacred Scriptures. That is the only way to free this woman. No amount of human rights is going to convince this woman steeped in religious tradition. You know what? *(Turning to the readers.)* I want you to wear a different pair of glasses and read some of the passages from your Scriptures which I am going to show you. *(Going closer to reader 1.)* Will you read this aloud?

Reader 1: *(Reluctantly.)* Galatians 3:28. "There is no longer Jew or Greek, there is no longer slave or free, there is no male or female; for all of you are one in Christ Jesus. And if you belong to Christ, then you are Abraham's offspring, heirs according to the promise."

Reader 2: It is me. I am a Jew. I am Abraham's offspring, according to promise.

Reader 3: I am a Muslim. I am also Abraham's offspring through his oldest son, Ishmael.

Reader 4: I am older than you are. I am older than all of you put together.

Reader 1: Older need not be better. *(Turning to reader 2.)* You know, I am the fulfillment of you, Judaism. That is what the text is talking about.

Reader 3: I am the youngest among us, Islam.

(Turning to readers 1 and 2.) I am the fulfillment of all of you.

Reader 4: You are not the youngest. There are more people out there who are not here today. For instance, my brother, Sikhism. He is younger than you are.

Detective: *(In the meantime, the detective unbinds the mouth of the woman.)* Do you have anything to say, woman, to these fighting men?

Woman: Thank you. It is nice to talk after all these years of silence. *(Turning to the readers.)* Brothers and sisters, if you are going to go by "juniority" and fulfillment, let me tell you something. Since Eve is created after Adam, she is a better version than man. That is, as a woman, I am a better version than you are, according to your own logic. But I am content with the verse, "There is no male or female in Jesus Christ." Women are neither superior nor inferior to men. We are equals.

Detective: Thank you. For a first-timer, that is a good speech. *(To reader 2.)* Now read this.

Reader 2: I realize now that there are two creation stories in the Torah. In Genesis 1:27, it says, "God created Adam" (which actually means humankind) "in His image. . . male and female He created them." In my Torah, someone tore this page by accident.

Detective: *(Unbinds the woman's eyes; speaks to the woman.)* What do you say to this?

Woman: Some of my brothers have had selective memory over the centuries. But I am so happy that my brothers and I are *equal* at last.

Detective: Are you sure? Let us see. *(To reader 3.)* Read this. You left out some verses from the Koran when you opposed woman's consent.

Reader 3: Surah 2:223: "Your wives are/As a tilth unto you/So approach your tilth/When or how you will; But . . . ."

Detective: This is an *important* "but." Go ahead.

Reader 3: "But do some good beforehand,/And fear God./And know that you are/To meet Him (in the Hereafter)./And give (these) good tidings to those who believe."

Detective: What does your creation story say?

Reader 3: Sura 53:45-46 in the Koran: "God did create/In pairs—male and female/ From a seed when lodged/In its place."

Detective: *(Unties the woman's hands.)* From the same source, God created both man and woman as equals. *(Detective toys with his glasses.)* Now reader 4. Read this from your Code of Manu.

Reader 4: "Where women are honored, there the gods are pleased, but where they are not honored, no sacred rite yields rewards. Where the female relations live in grief, the family soon perishes."[13]

Detective: *(Unties the woman's feet.)* Job accomplished. Now woman, what can I do for you?

Woman: Detective, can I have your glasses, please, for my reading?

Detective: Yes, you may have my glasses. *(To the readers.)* Do you all hear the bell? Now all of you and *(to the woman)* you, too, lady, go and do something to stop violence against women as an interfaith group. Goodbye, see you in the next School of Mission.

Discussion:

1. Lift up the models from chapter 4 of interfaith groups in various communities. Other models may come from United Methodist Women working on interfaith relations, e.g., "Interfaith Sisters" in Atlanta, Georgia, started in 1994 to discuss common concerns of women. It was initiated by Shan Yohan, a United Methodist woman currently serving as Women's Division director.

2. Small groups give reports on what their models are for interfaith communities.

Two-pronged commitment in creating interfaith communities:

1. (a) My engagement in dialogue involves being neighbor and (b) being a witness. What are some of the skills and tools, spiritual preparedness, and disciplines I need to strengthen and develop my ability to engage in these forms of dialogue?

2. Concrete action plans are necessary to build communities. Read chapter 5 of the study book. Come up with one model and accompanying concrete action plans to create interfaith awareness in your local church or UMW unit in order to build bridges in your larger community. Write them down and share with the entire group.

A common saying: "The Church is the only organization which exists for its nonmembers."

Commitment: Food for the Journey

(The facilitator should make ready three to four plates with table grapes or an orange on each of the plates. Make available some paper napkins also. Divide the class into three or four subgroups.

Give each subgroup a plate of table grapes or one orange for each of the subgroups.)

Facilitator:

I am going to read a passage from the Bible. Listen. Do not speak, please. When I read the passage, if you feel that a certain verse will be a blessing to your neighbor, feed that person with a grape or a piece of the orange. Such a feeding is messy. That is all right. But *do not* feed yourself. Feed each other. That is the basic requirement of this exercise.[14] Do it in silence. Keep enough paper napkins. But remember, getting messy as you feed others is okay. It is inevitable.

The facilitator reads aloud Matthew 5:1-16 slowly and meaningfully. If the group has not fed itself at the end of the passage, the facilitator repeats Matthew 5:13-16. At the end of this reading, the facilitator asks: How did you feel as you were fed by others? Happy? Humble?

(After sharing the experience, the facilitator tells the entire group that in this journey we feed each other, leaving out no one. Then the facilitator leads the entire group in the following litany.)

Litany: Grace for the Journey

Leader: Giver of grace, give us strength and sustenance for the task ahead.

All: God of second chances, give us a second wind for the journey ahead.

Leader: In our journey of being a people of God for all God's peoples.

All: In our mission of bridging our small world with God's larger family.

Leader: To be the salt of the earth.

All: To be the light of the world.

Leader: For you are at the heart of the earth.

All: For you are at the core of our very heavens.

Leader: Nudging us to taste the fullness of life.

All: Urging us to offer fullness of life to others.

Leader: Grant us the guidance of your Holy Spirit every step of our way.

All: Grant us your accompanying grace every minute of our lives.

Leader: For the sake of your dailiness of love.

All: For the sake of yet a closer walk with you and our neighbor.

Leader: We ask this in the name of the love of God, for the sake of the daily companionship of your Holy Spirit.

All: And in the name of the author and perfecter of this and each of our journeys, even Jesus the Christ. Amen.

Closing hymn: *The United Methodist Hymnal,* #593, "Here I Am, Lord."

Endnotes:

1. The phrase "Boundary-breaking God" is borrowed from a conversation with Kosuke Koyama, John D. Rockefeller Jr. Emeritus Professor of Ecumenical Studies, Union Theological Seminary, New York.

2. The idea of making a sticky wall is borrowed from education trainers Carol Barton and Elmira Nazombe.

3. For the list of pure and impure, we have relied on the Hebrew Scriptures as well as Rosemary Radford Ruether's *Women and Redemption: A Theological History* (Minneapolis: Fortress Press, 1998).

4. *A Wideness in God's Mercy: The Finality of Jesus Christ in World Religions* (Grand Rapids, Mich.: Zondervan, 1992), p. 141.

5. *The Gospel in a Pluralist Society* (Grand Rapids, Mich.: Eerdmans, 1989), p. 175.

6. Stanley Samartha, *One Christ—Many Religions: Towards A Revised Christology* (Maryknoll, N.Y.: Orbis Press, 1991), p.149.

7. The idea of a "scapecoat" is borrowed from Clarissa Pinkola Estes, *Women Who Run with the Wolves: Myths and Stories of the Wild Woman Archetype* (New York: Ballantine Books, 1992), pp. 385-386.

8. Christopher Duraisingh, ed. *Called to One Hope: The Gospel in Diverse Culture* (Geneva: World Council of Churches, 1998), p. 13.

9. "The problem of cooperation between foreign and native workers," by the Rev. V.S. Azariah in the World Missionary Conference in Edinburgh, Scotland, in 1910. Roger E. Headland, ed. *Roots of the Great Mission Debate in Mission: Mission in Historical and Theological Perspective* (Bangalore, India: Theological Book Trust), p. 48, citing pp. 42-48 from the Azariah report.

10. Blu Greenberg, "Female Sexuality and Bodily Functions in the Jewish Tradition," in Jeanne Becher, ed. *Women, Religion and Sexuality* (Geneva: World Council of Churches, 1990), pp. 4, 9.

11. Riffat Hassan, "An Islamic Perspective," *Women, Religion and Sexuality*.

12. Vasudha Narayanan, "Hindu Perceptions of Auspiciousness and Sexuality," *Women, Religion and Sexuality*, p. 72.

13. The idea of feeding each other while reading a Bible passage is taken from Megan McKennan, *Not Counting Women and Children* (Maryknoll, N.Y.: Orbis Books, 1994).

BIBLIOGRAPHY

Ariarajah, S. Wesley. *Not Without my Neighbour.* WCC Publications, 1999.

Ariarajah, S. Wesley. *The Bible and People of Other Faiths.* WCC Publications, 1985.

Ariarajah, S. Wesley. *Gospel and Culture.* WCC Publications, 1995.

Center for Democratic Renewal. *When Hate Comes to Town: A Handbook of Effective Community Responses.* 2001-2002. Third Edition. [Available from Service Center. 1-800-305- 9857. Fax: 1-513-761-3722. Price: $10.]

Dharmaraj, Glory. *Concepts of Mission.* New York: GBGM, 1999.

Dharmaraj, Jacob & Glory. *Christianity and Islam: A Missiological Encounter.* SPCK, Delhi: Cambridge Press, 1998. Second Edition 1999.

Dupuis, S.J. Jacques. *Jesus Christ at the Encounter of World Religions.* Maryknoll, New York: Orbis Books, 1989

Eck, L. Diana. *A New Religious America: How a 'Christian Country' Has Become the World's Most Religiously Diverse Nation.* New York, NY: Harper Collins Publishers, Inc., 2001.

Hambrick, Charles, et al. *Religions: Encountering People of Other Faiths.* To the Point Confronting Youth Issues. Nashville, TN: Abingdon Press, 1995.

Kateregga, D. Badru and Shenk, W. David. *A Muslim and a Christian in Dialogue.* Wateroll, Ontario: Herald Press, 1997.

Knitter, F. Paul. *One Earth, Many Religions.* Maryknoll, NY: Orbis Books, 1995.

Küng, Hans. *Christianity: Essence, History, and Future.* New York, NY: The Continuum Publishing Company, 2001.

Küng, Hans. *Christians and World Religions: Paths to Dialogue.* Maryknoll, NY: Orbis Books, 1993.

Mallon, Elias. *Neighbors: Muslims in North America.* New York: Friendship Press, 1989.

Musk, A. Bill. *Touching the Soul of Islam: Sharing the Gospel in Muslim Cultures.* Crowbourgh: Marc, 1995.

Neil, Stephen. *Christian Faith & Other Faiths.* Downers Grove, IL: InterVarsity Press, 1984.

Parrinder, Geoffrey. *Introduction to Asian Religions.* New York: Oxford University Press, 1957.

Peters, F.E. *A Reader on Classical Islam.* Princeton University Press: New Jersey: Princeton, 1994.

Raines, John C. *The Justice Men Owe Women: Positive Resources from World Religions.* Minneapolis, MN: Fortress Press, 2001.

Smith, Houston. *The World's Religions: Our Great Wisdom Traditions.* San Francisco: Harper, 1961.

Speight, R. Marston. *God is One: The Way of Islam.* New York: Friendship Press, 2001.

Thangaraj, M. Thomas. *Relating to People of Other Religions.* Nashville, TN: Abingdon Press, 1994.

VIDEOGRAPHY

Our Muslim Neighbors. Evangelical Lutheran Church of America, Division of Global Mission,. 8765 West Higgins Road, Chicago, IL 60631.

Faith & Belief: Five Major World Religions, 1992. Knowledge Unlimited Inc., P.O. Box 52, Madison, WI 53701.

Not In Our Town, 1995. California Working Group, 5867 Ocean View Drive, Oakland, CA 694618.

America's New Religious Landscape. Alban Institute, PO Box 211, Annapolis Junction, MD 20701.

CD-ROM

On Common Ground: World Religions in America. Dana L. Eck and the Pluralism Project. New York, NY: Columbia University Press, 1997. Phone: 1-800-944-8648.

POSTERS

1. 5 posters [Christianity, Hinduism, Buddhism, Judaism, & Islam]. Size each: 18" x 25". Stock #7088P. Price: $24.95. Individual poster, $5.95 each. Available from Knowledge Unlimited Inc., P.O. Box 52, Madison, WI 53701-0052. Phone: 1-800-356-2303.

2. Map & Timeline of World Religions. Stock #PE764. Size: 36" x 19". Price: $9.95. Available from Knowledge Unlimited, Inc.

3. "Celebrate Community & Honor Diversity." 18" x 24". Stock #P482CW. Price: $15. Available from Syracuse Cultural Workers, Tools for Change, P.O. Box 6367 Syracuse, NY 13217. Phone: 315-474-1132. Fax: 877-265-5399. E-mail: scw@syrculturalworkers.org. Website: www.syrculturalworkers.org.

4. "World Religion Map and Timeline." 18" x 25". Stock #7186P. Price: $14.95. Available from Knowledge Unlimited, Inc., P.O. Box 52, Madison, WI 53701-0052. Phone: 1-800-356-2303. Website: www.theKUstore.com.

APPENDICES

Christianity

Buddhism

Islam

Hinduism

Judaism

Jainism

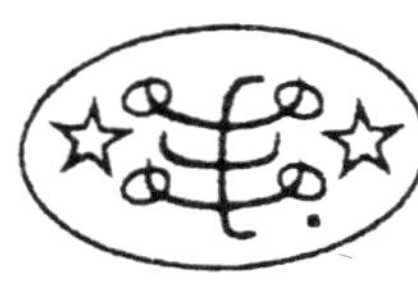

Baha'i Faith

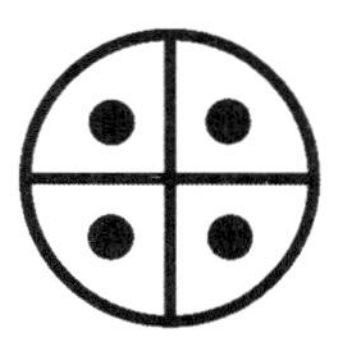

Native American Spirituality

Information taken from: *When Hate Comes to Town: A Handbook of Effective Community Responses 2001-2002, 3rd Edition.* Taylor Letter Service: Atlanta, GA.

Center for Democratic Renewal CDR National Office
P.O. Box 50469
Atlanta, GA 30301
Phone: 404.221.0025
Fax: 404.221.0045
Web: www.thecdr.org
Email: info@thecdr.org

AFL-CIO Civil Rights Department
815 16th St. NW
Washington, D.C. 20006
Phone: 202.637.5000
Fax: 202.637.5058
Web: www.aflcio.org
Email: rwomack@aflcio.org

American-Arab Anti-Discrimination Committee
4201 Connecticut Ave., NW
Suite 300
Washington, DC 20008
Phone: 202.244.2990
Fax: 202.244.3196
Web: www.adc.org
Email: adc@theadc.org

American Baptist Churches in the USA
P.O. Box 851
Valley Forge, PA 19482
Phone: 610.768.2000 /
       800.ABC.3USA
Web: www.abc-usa.org

American Friends Service Committee
1501 Cherry Street
Philadelphia, PA 19102
Phone: 215.241.7000
Fax: 215.241.7275
Web: www.afsc.org
Email: afscinfo@afsc.org

American Muslim Council
1212 New York Avenue, NW
Suite 400
Washington, DC 20005
Phone: 202.789.2262
Fax: 202.789.2550
Web: www.amconline.org
Email: amc@amconline.org

Anti-Defamation League of B'nai B'rth
823 United Nations Plaza
Suite 100
New York, NY 10017
Phone: 212.490.2525
Fax: 212.867.0779
Web: www.adl.org
Email: adl@adl.org

Anti-Racist Action
P.O. Box 82097
Columbus, OH 43202
Phone: 614.464.9074
Web: www.antiracistaction.org

Asian American Legal Defense and Education Fund
99 Hudson St., 12th Floor
New York, NY 10013
Phone: 212.966-5932
Web: www.aaldef.org

Asian Law Caucus
468 Bush St., 3rd Floor
San Francisco, CA 94108
Phone: 415.391.1655
Fax: 415.391.0366
Web: www.asianlawcaucus.org
Email: alc@asianlawcaucus.org

California Association of Human Relations Organizations
1426 Fillmore Street, Suite 216
San Francisco, CA 94414
Phone: 415.115.2341
Fax: 415.775.2342
Web: www.cahro.org
Email: info@cahro.org

Catholic Campaign for Human Development
3211 4th Street N.E.
Washington, DC 20017
Phone: 202.541.3210
Fax: 202.541.3329
Web: www.nccbuscc.org/cchd

Center for Community Change
1000 Wisconsin Ave. NW
Washington, DC 20017
Phone: 202.342.0519
Fax: 202.342.1132
Web: www.communitychange.org
Email: info@communitychange.org

Center for Constitutional Rights
666 Broadway, 7th Floor
New York, NY 10012
Phone: 212.614.6464
Fax: 212.614.6499
Email: ccr@igc.org

Center for New Community
PO Box 36066
Chicago, IL 60634
Phone: 708.848.0319
Fax: 708.848.0327
Web: www.newcomm.org
Email: newcomm@newcomm.org

Center on Hate and Extremism
5500 University Parkway
San Bernardino, CA 92407
Phone: 909.880.7711
Fax: 909.880.7025
Web: www.hatemonitor.org

Committee Against Anti-Asian Violence
121 6th Avenue, 6th Floor
New York, NY 10013
Phone: 718-220-7391
Fax: 718.220.7398
Web: www.caaav.org
Email: justice@caaav.org

The Episcopal Church, USA
815 Second Avenue
New York, NY 10017
Phone: 212.867.8400 /
        800.334.7626
Web: www.ecusa.anglican.org

Evangelical Lutheran Church in North America
8765 West Higgins Road
Chicago, IL 60631
Phone: 773.380.2700 /
        800.638.3522
Fax: 773.380.1465
Web: www.elca.org

Freedom of Information
FBI (Attn: FOI-PA Section)
9th and Pennsylvania Avenue
Washington, DC 20535
Phone: 202.324.5520
Fax: 202.324.3752
Web: http://foia.fbi.gov

Highlander Research Education Center
1959 Highlander Way
New Market, TN 37820
Phone: 865.933.3443
Fax: 865.933.3424
Web: www.highlandercenter.org
Email: hrec@highlandercenter.org

Lambda Legal Defense and Education Fund
120 Wall Street, Suite 1500
New York, NY 10005
Phone: 212.809.8585
Fax: 212.809.0055
Web: www.lambdalegal.org
Email:
        lambdalegal@lambdalegal.org

Lawyers Committee for Civil Rights Under Law
294 Washington Street, Suite 443
Boston, MA 02108
Phone: 617.482.1145
Fax: 617.482.4392
Email: office@lawyerscom.org

Leadership Conference on Civil Rights
1629 K Street NW
Washington, DC 20006
Phone: 202.466.3311
Fax: 202.466.3435
Web: www.civilrights.org

Maryland Commission on Human Relations
William Donald Schaefer Tower
6 St. Paul Street, Suite 900
Baltimore, MD 21202
Phone: 410.767.8600
Fax: 410.333.1841
Web: www.mchr.state.md.us
Email:
        mchr@mail.mchr.state.md. us

Mexican American Legal Defense Fund (MALDEF)
634 South Spring Street
11th Floor
Los Angeles, CA 90014
Phone: 213.629.2512
Fax: 213.629.0266
Web: www.maldef.org

National Association for the Advancement of Colored People (NAACP)
1025 Vermont Avenue, NW #1120
Washington, DC 20005
Phone: 202.638.2269
Fax: 202.737.8651
Web: www.naacp.org

National Asian Pacific American Legal Consortium
1140 Connecticut Avenue, NW
Suite 1200
Washington, DC 20036
Phone: 202.296.2300
Fax: 202.296.2318
Web: www.napalc.org
Email: sscanlon@napalc.org

National Center for Victims of Crime
2111 Wilson Blvd. Suite 300
Arlington, VA 22201
Phone: 703.276.2880
Fax: 703.276.2889
Web: www.ncvc.org

National Coalition for Burned Churches
PO Box 40784
Charleston, SC 29423
Phone: 843.853.5363
Fax: 843.853.5366
Web: www.ncfbc.org
Email: ncfbccp@aol.com

National Congress of Black Churches
2000 L Street, NW Suite 225
Washington, DC 20036
Phone: 202.296.5657
Fax: 202.296.4939
Web: www.cnbc.org

National Council of Churches of Christ in the USA
475 Riverside Drive
New York, NY 10115
Phone: 212.870.2227
Web: www.ncccusa.org

National Council of La Raza (NCLR)
1111 19th NW, Suite 1000
Washington, DC 20036
Phone: 202.785.1670
Fax: 202.776.1792
Web: www.nclr.org

National Gay and Lesbian Task Force
1700 Kalorama Road NW
Suite 101
Washington, DC 20009
Phone: 202.332.6483
Fax: 202.332.0207
Web: www.ngltf.org
Email: ngltf@ngltf.org

National Network for Immigrant and Refugee Rights
310 Eighth Street, Suite 310
Oakland, CA 94607
Phone: 510.465.1984
Fax: 510.465.1885
Web: www.nnirr.org
Email: nnirr@nnirr.org

National Spiritual Assembly of the Baha'is of the United States
1320 19th Street, Suite 701
Washington, DC 20036
Phone: 202.833.8990
Fax: 202.833.8988
Web: http://orgs.unt.edu/BFC/
       Intro_NSA.htm
Email: usnsa_oea@usnbc.org

Northwest Coalition for Human Dignity
PO Box 21428
Seattle, WA 98111
Phone: 206.762.5622
Fax: 206.762.5968
Web: www.nwchd.org
Email: nwhcd@nwhcd.org

Office of the Assistant Attorney General - Civil Rights Division
PO Box 65808
Washington, DC 20035
Phone: 202.514.2151
Fax: 202.514.0293
Web: www.usdoj.gov

Pennsylvania Human Relations Commission
Pennsylvania Place, Suite 300
301 Chestnut Street
Harrisburg, PA 17101
Phone: 717.787.4410
Fax: 717.787.0420
Web: www.phrc.state.pa.us

People Against Racist Terror (PART)
PO Box 1055
Culver City, CA 90232
Phone: 310.495.0299
Web: www.usdoj.gov
Email: part2001@usa.net

Political Research Associates
1310 Broadway, Suite 201
Somerville, MA 02144
Phone: 617.666.5300
Fax: 617.666.6622
Web: www.publiceye.org
Email: puliceye@igc.org

Prejudice Insitute/Center for the Applied Study of Ethnoviolence
2743 Maryland Avenue
Baltimore, MD 21218
Phone: 410.366.9654
Web: www.prejudiceinstitute.org
Email: prejinst@aol.com

Presbyterian Church (U.S.A.)
100 Witherspoon Street
Louisville, KY 40202
Phone: 502.569.5000
Fax: 502.569.5018
Web: www.pcusa.org

Progressive National Baptist Convention, Inc.
601 50th Street, NE
Washington, DC 20019
Phone: 202.396.0558
Fax: 202.398.4498
Web: www.pnbc.org

Religious Action Center of Reform Judaism
2027 Massachusetts Ave. NW
Washington, DC 20036
Phone: 202.387.2800
Fax: 202.667.9070
Web: www.rac.org
Email: rac@uahc.org

Simon Wiesenthal Center
9786 West Pico Boulevard
Los Angeles, CA 90049
Phone: 310.553.9036
Fax: 310.553.4521
Web: www.wisenthal.com

Southeast Regional Economic Justice Network
PO Box 240
Durham, NC 27707
Phone: 919.683.4310
Fax: 919.683.3428
Web: www.rejn.org
Email: serejn@rejn.org

Southern Christian Leadership Conference (SCLC)
334 Auburn Ave. NE
Atlanta, GA 30312
Phone: 404.522.1420
Fax: 404.659.7390
Email: sclchq@bellsouth.net

Southern Institute for Education and Research
MR Box 1692
31 McAlister Drive
New Orleans, LA 70118
Phone: 504.865.6100
Fax: 504.862.8957
Web: www.southerncatalyst.org

Southern Organizing Committee for Economic and Social Justice (SOC)
PO Box 10518
Atlanta, GA 30310
Phone: 404.755.2855
Fax: 404.755.0575
Web: http://igc.org/socejp
Email: socejp@igc.apc.org

Southern Poverty Law Center
400 Washington Avenue
Montgomery, AL 36104
Phone: 334.956.8200
Fax: 334.956.8485
Web: www.splcenter.org

Texas Freedom Network
PO Box 1624
Austin, TX 78767
Phone: 512.322.0545
Fax: 512.322.0550
Web: www.tfn.org

UAW Civil Rights Department
8000 East Jefferson Avenue
Detroit, MI 48214
Phone: 313.926.5461
Web: www.uaw.org
Email: uaw@uaw.org

Unitarian Universalist Association of Churches
25 Beacon Street
Boston, MA 02108
Phone: 617.742.2100
Fax: 617.367.3237
Web: www.uua.org

United Churches of Christ
700 Prospect Avenue
Cleveland, OH 44115
Phone: 216.736.3700
Fax: 216.736.3703
Web: www.ucc.org

United Methodist Church General Board of Global Ministries
475 Riverside Drive, Room 1400
New York, NY 10115
Phone: 212.870.3606
Fax: 212.870.3748
Web: www.gbgm-umc.org

United States Department of Justice
Hate Crime Hotline
Phone: 1.800.347.HATE (4283)

The Women's Project
2224 Main Street
Little Rock, AR
Phone: 501.372.5113
Fax: 501.372.6853
Web: www.womens-project.org
Email: wproject@aol.com

AUTHORS

Before his retirement in 1992, **the Reverend Dr. R. Marston** Speight was Director of the Office for Christian-Muslim Relations of the National Council of the Churches of Christ in the U.S.A. and a member of the adjunct faculty of Hartford Seminary. Prior to those appointments he served as a missionary in North Africa from 1951 until 1979. He pastored churches in Algiers, Algeria and Tunis, Tunisia and lectured in a number of countries of Europe, the Middle East and Africa. He has authored, coauthored and translated several books. Dr. Speight is an ordained minister in The United Methodist Church and lives with his family in Connecticut.

Glory E. Dharmaraj, Ph.D., is Executive Secretary for Justice Education for the Women's Division, General Board of Global Ministries of The United Methodist Church. She is also the administrator of the Seminar Program on National and International Affairs at the Church Center for the United Nations. Glory currently serves on the Board of Directors of Scarritt Bennett Center, Nashville, Tennessee, and the Foundation for Theological Education in South East Asia. She has written books on *Concepts of Mission* and *Christmas People in a Terrorist Crisis.*

She has co-authored two books with her husband, a United Methodist clergyperson: *Christianity and Islam: A Missiological Encounter* and *Mutuality in Mission.*

Jacob S. Dharmaraj, Ph.D., was born and raised in India. He was ordained in Bombay Annual Conference in 1976. Currently, he serves as pastor at the Shrub Oak United Methodist Church in the New York Annual Conference. He has published numerous academic articles and three books. He has served churches in the Bombay Annual Conference and the Illinois Great River Conference. His most recent book, which he co-authored with Glory, is *Mutuality in Mission.*

Seven Friends – Seven Faiths. By Martha Bettis Gee. This storybook with photo cubes tells of children of different faiths and how they celebrate their faith. Christian, Jewish, Muslim, Hindu, Sikh, Buddhist, and Baha'i children explain to those of other faiths what their holidays mean. The nine photo cubes, which are a put-together project, illustrate the various faith celebrations.

(#03287) $4.00, 5 for $15.00, 10 for $25.00

Seven Friends – Seven Faiths Teacher's Guide. By Martha Bettis Gee. This guide helps children learn about our rich interfaith community by learning about the celebrations of different faiths including our own. It offers three sessions for children aged 6 through 12 and an intergenerational experience including games, recipes, songs, and stories. Each session begins with worship, and the Bible study has a wide variety of activities for different age levels.

(#03288) $6.00

Youth Study – Who Is The Kid Next Door? Creating Interfaith Community, including **Leader's Guide.** By Kelly Martini. Younger Christians are growing up in an increasingly interreligious world. They go to school and live in communities with others from Hindu, Muslim, Jewish, and other faiths. They see religious conflicts in the news on a daily basis. And they question whether their Christian faith is mature enough to engage in dialogue and live in harmony with those of other faiths. This is a book of stories told by youth from a variety of religious backgrounds about quests for peace and justice in our world through which they learn about each other. These stories will engage youth in discussions on interfaith issues, on personal faith journeys as Christians, and on a quest to live with others in an interreligious community. This resource can be used in classrooms, retreats, or youth group settings.

(#03289) $6.00

Please mail order with check payable to:
SERVICE CENTER
PO BOX 691328
CINCINNATI OH 45269-1328

Costs for shipping and handling for sale items:
$25 or less, add $4.65
$25.01-$60, add $5.75
$60.01-$100, add $7.00
Over $100, add 6.5%

Revised formula effective March 15, 2002.

For billed and credit card orders:
CALL TOLL FREE: 1-800-305-9857
If billing is requested, a $1.50 billing fee will be added.
FAX ORDERS: 1-513-761-3722
E-MAIL: SCorders@gbgm-umc.org

SERVICE CENTER
7820 READING RD CALLER NO 1800
CINCINNATI OH 45222-1800

$7.50   **Stock #03286**